S0-AHD-717

BV
4012
.T483   Thilo
            Unfragmented man

Date Due

WITHDRAWN
by Unity Library

UNITY SCHOOL LIBRARY
Unity Village
Lee's Summit, Missouri 64063

PRINTED IN U.S.A.

UNFRAGMENTED MAN

UNFRAGMENTED MAN

A Study in Pastoral Psychology

by

HANS–JOACHIM THILO

Translated from the German
by
ARTHUR J. SEEGERS

WITHDRAWN
by Unity Library

UNITY SCHOOL LIBRARY
Unity Village
Lee's Summit, Missouri 64063

AUGSBURG PUBLISHING HOUSE
MINNEAPOLIS   MINNESOTA

UNFRAGMENTED MAN

Copyright © 1964 Augsburg Publishing House

All rights reserved

Library of Congress Catalog Card No. 64-13433

Translated from *Der ungespaltene Mensch*. Ein Stück Pastoral-psychologie
by Hans-Joachim Thilo. Published in 1957 in Göttingen, Germany,
by Vandenhoeck & Ruprecht

MANUFACTURED IN THE UNITED STATES OF AMERICA

This English edition
is dedicated
in love and gratitude
to
my friend and brother
in trying days
the Reverend E. H. Robertson,
Yeovil, England

FOREWORD

"And the Word became flesh and dwelt among us, full of grace and truth; we have beheld his glory, glory as of the only Son from the Father" (John 1:14).

In the study scene of *Faust* Goethe gives his opinion that the Word should not possibly be rated so highly as to be placed at the very beginning of all things. He says that the Word must yield first place to the deed. Goethe was a comprehensive thinker, the last of our epoch; but the Word-become-flesh remained for him a hidden fact. How greatly he was impelled by a craving for objectification of the ineffable is evident both from his doctrine of color and from his *West-Easterly Divan*. It may be that in our time of confusion men are similarly motivated. We probably can understand them best by saying that they are striving mainly to see and to grasp the mysteries of God. They have had experience with these mysteries of God so palpably in judgment and preservation. This is the same as to say that among us there is an experience like that of Goethe. Among us also there is the same remarkable split of intention. On the one hand, tremendous store is set by the inquiring mind. On the other hand, there is the tendency to stop short of going into the area of the essential *(das Eigentliche)*, to which, by the grace of God, entrance may be had. But so long as this world stands, man can gain entry into the realm of the essential only where God's Word-become-flesh *is* the way, the truth, and the life. Note well: *is*, not shows or brings or means. Therefore this book purports to be a cautious effort at assessing the questions which exercise our minds as we care for souls in our day. Here the assessment is made in the context of God's gift of the *Deus Incarnatus*. Significantly, the traditional liturgy of the mass has no music at the passage *"et homo factus est,"* and it has the priest stand in silent adoration before the altar. We know that we can add nothing to this deed of

6

God, neither by speaking nor by writing. But as God enables us, we may recognize and bear witness to the lordship of Christ in all areas of creation. In this book the aim is to draw from the Second Article and then clarify the laws of creation as these come within the province of the First Article and are operative in soul-care and in services of worship. This pastoral effort will provoke various kinds of criticism. Contradiction, though, can only be helpful. Contradictors should be careful not to hurl word missiles in an effort to wipe out things whose reality is evident each day and hour. Such words could be: magic, gnosticism, or sacramentalism. Diagnoses of our time we have had in all areas to the point of surfeit. It is time to turn to therapy. A part of this therapy has to be that the insights gained outside of theology be made useful in theology. We should be ready to admit that the Lord of all can direct the hearts of men as waterbrooks even without benefit of churchly vocabulary and theological concepts. It follows from the fact that God dwells among men that our encounter with the world becomes a duty. "Confrontation makes for healing," is what the psychiatrists say. Would that we might recognize this from the very beginning of our work in the church. God confronts us, and we confront each other. The church faces the world. The visible faces the invisible. Werner Bergengruen has said that we grow in the same degree in which the invisible becomes visible for us.

I owe thanks to all who in numerous counseling sessions have given me their confidence, among them especially children and youth. My thanks go very especially to the man who has become my spiritual father, to whom I dedicate this book, the *Kirchenrat* Alfred Fritz of Berlin-Teltow, and to my wife for many hours of quiet fellowship. Also, and not least, my thanks should go to coworkers in the child guidance center of the church connected with the Inner Mission in Berlin, and to those who helped with technical matters in the production of the book: Mrs. Welke, Miss Hagen, and Miss Bartels who helped in recent months. Standing above the concurrence or contradiction which this work will occasion is the witness of Holy Scripture, "In him we live and move and have our being."

HANS-JOACHIM THILO

CONTENTS

INTRODUCTION: RELATIONSHIP BETWEEN THEOLOGY AND PSYCHOLOGY

The intellectual mold of the last 300 years was shaped by the dialogue between theology and the specific branches of science that theology had to reckon with. In the 17th and 18th centuries the dialogue was with philosophy, in the 19th with historiography, and in the 20th with the natural sciences. Fluid as were the boundaries of the periods of time, so various also were the degrees of attention which now and then the parties to the dialogue accorded each other.

At the turn of the century the dominant questions were still those posed to theology by Haeckel and Darwin. After World War I there was a sharp increase in the number of questions raised by medicine as a branch of natural science. It seemed as though branch after branch of medicine unexpectedly got into the dialogue with theology. At first somatic medicine evinced little interest in this engagement. The laws operative in it seemed so incontrovertible proven, and convincing that only one question could be asked by theology: whether and in what sense somatic medicine could justify itself as a science. A genuine question is posed for theology when there is a development in medicine that gets out of control. Depth psychology—and that is what we mean by psychology in this book —took its beginning as clinical psychology. The discovery of it was made in clinical therapy. This occurred when the therapeutic measures which had been so confidently employed in pure somatic turned out to be but partially valid. What today is called psychosomatic medicine owes its origin, not to philosophical inquiry concerning medicine, but rather to a developmental breakthrough within its own ranks. V. Bergmann put it this way, "I mean to show that by the new thinking in medicine we are intent upon reckoning with evaluations, as was the case in the Hippocratic age; we do not content ourselves with mere neutral, objective description of the observed, but we dare to evaluate it. . . . We have come to the insight that in accordance with the principle of function we must combine the activities of the several organs into organ-systems and arrive at spheres of functioning" (*Neues Denken in der Medizin,* p. 7).

What develops cannot be ignored by the other sciences when the evolution of medicine begins to turn in a performance like that of an apprentice magician and the conjured spirits (as in the 20's) make as though they would topple the whole structure of organic medicine. Thus it was not by chance that theology, at that same time, made a beginning with what among us is called "new considerations in theology." At the same time that theology discovered that God would have to remain the God who in the dialectic between *absconditus* and *revelatus* reveals his secrets nowhere else than in Word and Sacrament, medical men were engaged in drawing conclusions from the fact that man is not only body but also soul and spirit.

This was a revolution in the field of medicine. The revolt was against Virchow's claim that man cannot possibly have a soul because operative explorations had turned up no trace of a soul, and the turn was to books like Heyer's *Praktische Seelenkunde* and Pfahler's *Der Mensch und seine Vergangenheit.* Related branches of medical science have taken too little cognizance of this revolution in medicine. What we have is no longer merely some specialized interests of a few learned men in a department. It is a process that encompasses all of medicine. To be sure, this reconsideration in medicine does not by any means go unchallenged, and it has not gotten through to all the doctors. It is important to point out that in this medical reconsideration really nothing new is being brought forth. It is simply a case of rediscovering what in medicine can be paraphrased with the name of Paracelsus. The thing is really a rediscovery of the connections between creation and the creature and of the medical responsibility in face of these two entities. In all that transpires in medicine, the most disquieting and yet promising event is this turning from a purely material principle to a recognition of a psychical and mental principle. Should it not be disquieting to realize that the human being is known only by half when no more than his anatomical and organic affinities are comprehended?

Marginally it may be noted that in philosophy a very similar turn has been taken. Kierkegaard about marks the finish of rational critical possibilities and of the meaningfulness of every a priori. And so, in modern inquiry concerning the existence of man, nothing is clearer than that man as such can be neither the object nor the center of philosophical consideration; he can be seen only as part and parcel of the cosmos. Marx and materialism start here with the theory of the influence of the world around us. In his provocative book *Die Achse der Natur* (The Axis of Nature) Hans Blüher professes to see relationship of man to the cosmos only in the God-man relationship. And classical existentialism, reckoning with the same facts, derives from them the utter loneliness of man and a resulting absurdity. The whole concern is with man's position in the cosmos. And this is the question that theology must face.

In terms of dogmatics we would say that whereas the First Article has rationalistically been emptied of its content by the Enlightenment and above all by Positivism, there is in theology today a rediscovery of the Second Article. Hans Blüher would say that the axis has begun to show. The Second Article empowers the church to recognize anew her dialectic, her existence, and her message and to proclaim that message to the world. Thence comes her freedom when the church sees herself confronted by the visible powers of the world. The law of all revolutionary developments, however, is like that of the pendulum. Thus it happens that in theology and medicine the pendulum now threatens to swing out so far that necessary insights of the past are either not held to at all or not held in sufficient depth.

In medicine, currently, the question has become acute: Is psychosomatic medicine not well along on the way toward forgetting the somatic and thus toward falling victim to a philosophic animism which routinely ignores a valid body of knowledge taught in medical schools?[1] In theology we sense more and more that, with the new consideration of the Second Article, the First is pushed into the background, and we pursue the rediscovery of the Third Article hesitantly in our day. Here is where the inquiring parties can meet: theology, medicine, and philosophy. Philosophy has gone along with theology for centuries, but now it makes the astonishing claim that it has lost interest in being a party to the inquiry. So now, in its stead, we confer with natural science wherever it is concerned with the same object with which we are, namely the human being. Thus the question of the place of man in the cosmos is also a question of the image of man, of anthropology.

Suddenly the alignment of natural science with reference to abstract science, as this has prevailed since Erasmus, has changed. The sciences no longer stand over against each other in an either-or relationship. The cleavage between "exact" science and abstract science, by which "proof" becomes a shibboleth of science as such, has become a matter of little interest. After the end of the last war Helmuth Thielicke could formulate the "questions which Christendom addresses to the modern world." The solidarity of perplexity brackets all the sciences.

Appearances here are deceptive though. The encounter of the spirits has not resulted in universality. It is true that from the natural sciences men and ideas are coming to the fore that earnestly ask questions concerning God. It is also true that technical people of our day are beginning to dread the boundless freedom that has come to them. Consequently the once comfortable *orbis Christiana* has been displaced by fragmentation which extends from the split monad to the inability in art to compose a decent portrait. We are verily forced to pause and, as we move forward, to find our way back. This is a process at which we have only made a start. We are not yet done with the classical world picture of the natural

sciences as it was given shape by the Enlightenment. The question
concerning the totality of the universe has indeed been put again,
but the answer is not given anywhere. Theology that is given to
reflection should know this. Theology should not act as though it
had the stone of the wise in its hand by repeating some old formulations or by taking the struggle for actuality to be the solution of
the problem. We seem to be on the way from yesterday to tomorrow, but this way must still be negotiated through today.

It appears to us that the declaration in the Gospel of John that
the Word became flesh holds the necessary key to the problem. It
does not make a rational entity of the cosmos, nor does it relate
the cosmos to magic. It does not reduce man to mere body nor to
a "brained animal" (Brunner). And it does not let the world fall victim to materialistic absolutism. Luther writes, "Scriptures divide
man into three parts . . . and comparable to these three the whole
man is also, in another way, divided into two parts. . . . This other,
the soul, is exactly the same as spirit in nature, but in another function." The spirit is "the house in which faith and God's Word dwell";
the soul is that which "gives life to the body."[2]

It is only when man is seen as being triadic that theology and
medicine can consult with each other concerning him and do their
respective duties toward him. The immediate place of meeting
for this consultation is in pastoral counseling. Poimenics and her-
meneutics are no more separable from other disciplines of theology
than depth psychology is separable from medicine. Thus pastoral
counseling and depth psychology are the two children about whom
the parents are contending as to whether their children are to be
wedded, to be friends with each other, or whether they had better
turn their backs on each other. That is why the dialogue about pastoral care and psychology cannot be carried on by technicians of
these branches of work. This dialogue must concern itself with the
given factors on which the "parents" base their existence. There
appears to be a decadence in the thinking of our time. And when
it is averred that its complete breakdown is imminent, the reason
given for this usually is the loss of things which heretofore seemed
to stand firm. But there remains a cheering fact, a fact which we

can ascribe only to the grace of God. This fact is the totally new point of departure for the dialogue between the natural sciences and theology, particularly between medical doctors and pastors.

Happily, this kind of consultation is now widely done. Lectures, academy sessions, and discussions on psychotherapy and pastoral care (Seelsorge) are given an alarmingly large place on the "program." But the point on which the whole enterprise turns is often forgotten—namely, that lines must be drawn as these are indicated by the fact that God has become man. These lines must mark out the whole realm of theology as well as the whole realm of medicine. From this same point of vantage we should dare to say to the theologians, in a somewhat high-sounding and daring formulation: The thing is that we have a cosmic theology.[3] God's having become man is visible evidence of his having taken possession of all the visible and invisible realms of the world. If we live and move and have our being in him, then this obviously means something more than that an individual human being tarries at a specific place on earth for a period of say 70 years and there exercises what freedom he has in making decisions.

This something more goes beyond the individual's relationship to God, to which his right must by no means be challenged. This something more is the place of man in the processes of the cosmos as his place is derived from his relationship to God. Man lives primarily by his responsibility to God. The Bible has it that this responsibility takes two directions within man's existence. For one, man is to make the earth subject unto himself. This is his position in the universe. For the other, man has the assignment of letting the consequences of the love which God has bestowed upon him work themselves out on himself and on men around him. This is his position in society. Both areas of assignment inevitably lead to guilt. This is because man, of himself, cannot measure up to the requirements of the law addressed to him. Of the resultant guilt man is "sick" in a real sense. That is why there is need for healing. This healing comes from the place whence man was put into this tension.

In order to effect this healing in depth, God himself becomes man. He does this in such a way as to include lordship over creation. In pictured representations of God's becoming man the Christ-child sometimes holds the orb of the earth in his hand. He who lies in Mary's bosom is at the same time he whom the whole round world never enfolded. Christ is the *pantocrator* even on Golgotha and the cross. This is the real mystery of the world. By reason of it the relationship of psychology and pastoral care to each other always turns on the implications of the incarnation. Whether it occurs in the visible or in the invisible world, there is no event that is outside the hands of Mary's child.

Questions concerning the demarcation of the areas of the visible and the invisible are quite necessary; moreover, they are close at hand. When physician and pastor are free to see that their action is under the royal rulership of God, each will of himself understand what his limitations are and what his sober responsibility is.

But since we know that we have not yet advanced to the indicated point, we must still attempt to mark out the boundaries. The lines will have to be drawn where pastor, psychotherapist, and physician must say what each proposes to do. What makes it more difficult for each to say this is that in our time it is not clear whether and to whom such an accounting should be given. That is our difficulty. We cannot countenance a mixing of psychology and pastoral counsel. And we must warn against juggling with such concepts as priestly physician and the pastor's office of healing. God be praised for the men who have already achieved a synthesis. But sober clarity is mandatory. For its sake we shall have to continue to insist that the children of the parents walk side by side, join hands, and learn from each other as there is interplay of their respective endeavors. We still walk on separate paths though they be parallel paths. But in infinity parallels do intersect.

Experience teaches that when we attend to unavoidably necessary scientific detail work, it dawns on us how irresponsible it is on either side to blur even minor boundary lines. That is why the pastor is urgently warned from the start in this book against asking questions in pastoral counseling that have psychoanalytical intent. Questions about dreams can be included here. More than once latent schizophrenic bents have become manifest in apparently "harmless" counseling. Certainly, this can also happen to the psychotherapist or the psychiatrist. The difference is that he knows what must be done in the case while, with the best of intentions, the pastor cannot know. With equal emphasis we request of medical doctors who engage in psychotherapy that they do not operate with concepts of guilt and of feelings of sin until they have first let themselves be instructed on the basic difference between these two concepts and on the theological basis for dealing with them.

The dialogue between psychology and pastoral care means to disclose the whole complex of forces to which the human being is exposed in the cosmos. Far and wide, this effort puts us into a new frontier. Precisely in this effort we shall have to proceed in a genuinely scientific manner in the years ahead. We will correct many things, learn new things, and discard many things. But a beginning in this is so necessary that we must not delay it any longer.

This is true particularly in Germany. Holland meanwhile has its own chair in pastoral psychology. In Scandinavian lands, particularly in Denmark, service experience in psychiatric clinics is a required part in the training of pastors, as is attendance at lectures held by specified doctors in the medical college. In Germany, by and large, we still stand skeptically aloof. There is good reason for this. After a manner peculiar to us, much has been said and written on the subject during the last ten years that had little foundation and was rather fanciful.

It seems to me that theology and medicine still stand in an alignment to each other that dates from the Middle Ages, but that in the previous century the gap between them was made a deep gulf. Both contributed to this. Thus it is time for free conferences and joint counseling. Really, there has been no lack of these. But we must attempt to draw some initial conclusions. These may indeed frighten some on both sides. But life moves on and hardly allows us to stay on the safe side. We must take risks.

PART I

*The Man
to Whom
We Proclaim*

THE CHILD

Jesus often pointed to the child as exhibiting the standard in certain attitudes in a Christian's faith. In doing this, Jesus did not idealize the child nor make him a specimen for the psychologist. It should also be understood that Jesus did not intend for an adult to be infantile in any of his behavior. The fact remains that, by and large, his ministry centered in the child and in the sick person. We cannot beat capital out of this fact for psychology or theology. We want only to have it as a proper point of departure as we set out to study the development of the human being. We think that nature suggests the phases to be studied; also we think that love demands regard for these phases.

We begin with the child. From daily contact with children we should be well acquainted with their ways. But we observe that people who rear children often have mistaken notions about them. Here is a lad of five dressed in trousers and tie suitable for a grown man. A girl of five wears a dress as for a ball, her hair done in a permanent wave. If we were able to adapt our practice to the child as he is, we would do differently with him.

Also observable is the crudeness of parents, pastors, and teachers as they go about the spiritual nurture of children. One is almost amused, for they act as though children were miniature adults. The fact is that every child is altogether a child, and an individual at that. Child psychology tells us this. The child's body, soul, and spirit are entirely on the child's level of existence. This is also the biblical view of the child. Hence we must reckon with the fact that the moral world of the child is just as far removed from that of the adult as are his capacities of body and mind. What is good and bad, truthful and false, neat and unkempt—in short, the whole scale of values is on a different level for the child than for the adult. This, to be sure, does not preclude that in a given case the same ethical concepts are applicable to child and adult alike. But we must not heedlessly impose the morals of the adult on the child.

Every treatment of child psychology that attempts to be valid marks out definite periods in the child's development. The Bible also speaks of the gradual development of the child. Groh, Bühler, and Remplein have made this clear. We shall, therefore, have to be aware of certain periods in a child's life. There are, for instance, the periods of negative response *(Trotzalter)*. These are as discernible as is the age of the suckling. Granted. But we must take each child as he is. Factors that impinge upon the child may cause a mix-up in the phases of his development. The social milieu may do this. Biological and psychological factors play a part, and too often there are psychopathological distortions of the child's life. Thus, at his age, a child may have similarities with other children, yet stand apart from them rather markedly.

The results of psychological research forbid that we start the life story of a human being with his birth. This story begins when the mother first notices movements of the fetus. Proofs are not final, but the likelihood is strong that prenatal influences are of consequence for the whole of life. And there is no denying the fact that experience at birth is soul-shaking and soul-shaping. This is true aside from the unusual, accidental violence that may attend birth. A feeling of fear comes from being forced and pressed; then there is the change of climate, the sensing of light and other experiences at birth. These are not items of heredity. Hereditary factors must not be minimized. But wider recognition should be given to the fact that the first four years of life are of great importance in the formation of the child's self. Was there a warm, accepting atmosphere in the home? Were mother and child together? Did the birth of the second child occur too early for the first? How was the child fed? Any number of such factors have a determinative influence on the child's development.[1]

Father and mother may want either to hasten or to retard the development of their child.

Parents who aim to speed up their child's progress are apt to force him in toilet-training, walking, and talking. The little victim of this pressure is likely to react to it in protest during a later period. Not a few are bed wetters because they were toilet-trained too early. Later lack of concentration can often be traced to the fact that the earlier play period was cut short. The child will not be denied being a child. When parents cannot accept the little one as he is, it can only be harmful for the child.

On the other hand, there are parents who retard the child and attempt to keep him childish. They do this out of fear of their own aging. They stunt the child mentally, emotionally, and also organically. It is the parents' doing when a boy wears feminine curly locks and a girl of seven is dressed like a boy; each instance betrays the wish of parents to have had a child of the opposite sex. The child is then treated in a way that is psychologically wrong. But we also see parents demurring at the purpose that God has for us and our children. There are points at which psychology has something definite to say. This it does when children arrive at their first negative response stage in life, between the years of two and four. To break the will of a man is the province of God only. These are God's children, not ours; that is why we may not keep up the practices that have been usual during the child's negative response years. This behavior is an outward expression of inner development. Also, when the child begins to speak of himself in the first person rather than in the third, a significant event has taken place. The child has become a person.

It is true that every living thing has its own dignity at the moment of its origin, but the special dignity of a human being becomes evident precisely at this juncture in life. The child's "I will" marks his distinctive dignity as a creature of God, and it must not be countered by the equally stubborn "I will" of an adult. The evidence of will in the child must be welcomed, for the life of man in God's creation moves in "responsible society" as the World Council at Amsterdam put it. It follows that the purpose of education must be to form habits and to make for conforming behavior, but not in such a way as to break the will of the child. In educational practice methods will have to be devised that are in keeping with positive regard for the person of the child.[2]

Psychologically viewed, faulty treatment of the child in the negative response period has its bad results. Hidden aggression is one. And often incipient delinquency is discernible. This breaks out then in the later dissenting period, say around 12 and 14. Figuratively put, stern effort to break the child's will erects a dam behind which energy piles up. At the moment when the child surmises that he is physically equal to grown persons, the dam breaks.

Harking back to the first negative reply period, we should note that at this time the child craves contact with persons other than the parents. This craving needs to be satisfied. Pronounced withdrawal from others is abnormal behavior. By it parents may assess their own effectiveness as educators. The child's own choice of playmate may not accord with the wish of his teachers. This may be so throughout childhood and youth. But it is a mistake to intervene hastily. The child needs what he craves. What happens is that the strictly reared child feels attracted to the child of an opposite kind of rearing. Parents and teachers then speak of inferiority feelings. The fact is that moral concepts of the child are not on the level with those of adults. What appears unseemly, brash, filthy, and offensive to adults is of interest to the child because he has had no experience with it.

Nowadays the place where children and youth make contact with other persons is on the street. In spite of the dangers to the mental, emotional, and physical life that lurks there, it must not be ignored that the street is the world in which life is lived. To keep persons off the street and isolated from life there means to make hothouse plants of them. Then, when they must later, say during maturation, negotiate life on the street, they will suffer a degree of psychological shock. Life on the street is a sampling of the world in which God became man. To keep the young away from it may be showing contempt for the very creation of God which he loved and for which he gave himself. The way to do it is to affirm existence by becoming engaged with the world here and now. Both child and adult can do this by trusting in the Lord who overcame the world.

The child encounters the realities of the world and the fairy tale at the same time. The former demands the latter. In the view of the adult the two seem not to go together, but the child needs both. The fairy tale serves as a buffer between the child and the hard realities of life. It is not correct to equate the fairy story with fiction. C. G. Jung settled that. His discovery of the collective unconscious has been given its due in psychology; and now we can say that the fairy story is a component that fits the level of the child's biological development. The fairy story mirrors the child's longing to grow up, to conquer time and space, to gain experience. It also mirrors fear of experiences that the child is sure to have. The child may be only vaguely aware of the tension that prevails between him and his parents, yet he is eager for the portrayal of this situation in the story of the "stepmother" or in that of the parent ravens, as in Hansel and Gretel. The fairy story yields satisfactions about attitudes of the parents beyond his ability to understand. The child soul needs the fairy story as he needs air for his lungs or the tenderly stroking hand.

The growing youth for his part needs the folk tale. In the psychology of youth mention is sometimes made of the Siegfried or Brunhilde years. The story tells of the fight with the dragon, or of the departure from the parental home. It expresses youth's desire to master self and the world. Another story reflects youth's longing to win the favor of a lady who will indicate with rose or glove that her favor has been won. Seen in this context, Schiller's *Glocke* is a masterpiece at portraying the several stages of a human being's development.

We must reckon with the fact that as the child moves into the world of the fairy tale he also makes his first contact with the realm of religion. This comes about at services of worship, in church school, and, hopefully, in the home where children ask questions and parents give answers. Strange as this may seem to grown-ups, the child makes quite the same of the world of the Gospels as he does of the world of the fairy tales. These worlds lie on the same level for the child of from three to five. Instances are little Red Riding Hood and the wolf, the Lord Jesus and the children. It is important to know this.

At ten the child will give up the fairy tale, and he may give up the biblical story as well. When it dawns on the child that all this about the Easter rabbit, Santa Claus, the Sleeping Beauty, and of the stork are inventions of men, then the story of God and the truths of the Gospel are apt to be construed to be inventions of the same sort. A degree of confusion can be forestalled if the teacher will avoid saying, "Now I'll tell you a story," say about Jesus stilling the storm. "Story" connotes fable, and fable connotes that which is not true. With this in mind, we can understand why our confirmands will be attentive to Bible stories and yet not be deeply moved by them. It is necessary to bridge the gap between language used in religious instruction and the language that the child uses in other discourse. Moreover, it must be borne in mind that the child has a way of slipping into the pattern of thought in which he moves comfortably at his stage of development. How can we command his attention to the matter in hand? One way to do it is to mark the occasion especially. Light a candle, sing a hymn; somehow impress upon the child that now we are treating something special.

In catechetical instruction, terms that have currency in fairy tales should be avoided or, if used, explained. Examples are king, father, redemption, grace, and others. The child is disposed to misunderstand them according to their usage in the fairy tale. One may not even assume that the concept of father will be understood fully.

Take the case of Kurt, 21 years old, brought in for psychotherapy. He was seriously disturbed emotionally and depressed. Interviews disclosed hostility toward the church and every representation of God. He had quit the church and joined an assortment of groups avowedly opposed to the church. The review of his past experience revealed severe conflict with his father, who was an asocial person. As a child Kurt had often seen his father beat his mother and had himself been tortured by his father. The pastor reported that the lad had attended church school for a while but then quit rather suddenly; however, he had voluntarily attended children's services from his seventh to his tenth year. During the course of treatment Kurt one day began to sing hymns to himself. By this he clearly indicated religious associations. Then, as treatment progressed, he came to a crisis, and religious experiences were prominent.

But at the same time his sharp hostility also broke out. What had happened? The hatred of his father, which he could not get rid of, was projected onto the Father in heaven. This could be because God had been spoken of as Father without any mention of the fact that earthly fathers can give a false impression of a true father. It may be assumed that this crass instance may have sundry variations over a rather broad field when diagnosis is made of contemporary youth.

Necessary as familiarity with the fairy world is, an encounter with the lie about the stork is not necessary. Granting that Santa Claus and the Easter rabbit are genuine symbols, the stork must not be credited with being the same. This swamp fowl would appear to stand in a different context. Somehow it is associated in the psyche of grown-ups with unconscious sexual repression which has dislocated and degraded the properly erotic in their lives to the level of the foul swamp that is the habitat of the stork. There is no way of defending the stork story. The dignity that man has by reason of his co-creative capacity forbids that the Christian teacher speak in derogatory terms of the mystery of birth and growth. While sexuality is still latent in the child he will listen to explanations of the biological events of generation and birth on about the same level as he would listen to explanations of the function of an electric motor. Prompt preparation for marriage—and this is something quite different from the "enlightening" of past practice—will spare the child premature sexual excitement that is sure to be detrimental.

On the method of telling children about biological functions of the body a series of eminent writings have appeared. Special mention should be made of Dr. Otto Kersten's *Geschlechtliche Erziehung und Aufklärung,* Ferdinand Enke-Verlag, Stuttgart.[3]

The question may be asked, When does a child cease being a child distinctively? The answer is tied to what the New Testament says on the nature of the child. The repeated advice of Jesus to be like children and his pointing to the mind of the child are quite different from the idealizing of the child that we are so prone to now. The New Testament does not belittle the child or hold him of no account, nor does it say anything of hedging in the child or of making too strong demands on him. For Jesus the distinctive disposition of the child is simply his obvious and unfailing readiness to trust. Only the child can trust completely; only the child can accept fully and be altogether receptive to gifts. When the father-child relationship is right, the child will make trips with his father, be dead tired upon arrival at a city, yet not suspect that the two may have lost their way nor want to ask if the father knows where he is going. *At the hand of the father the child goes into the dark with all confidence. This trust marks the child as child.* Once this trust is gone, being a child has also ceased.

Operating with this fact, the evangelical psychologist will not measure childhood by any biological facts nor by empirical findings of a psychological sort. In our interviews we meet persons of 20 years who are truly children, persons of 15 years whom parents have stunted to remain children, and persons of 10 years who, by reason of their experiences, exhibit behavior and mental traits of adults. The stereotypes that were employed in psychology at the turn of the century have long since been called in question, likewise the grading by age of a later day is suspect if it is made with no refer-ence to the wisdom of the Word of God relative to the nature of the child.

THE YOUTH

We have noted as the distinctive mark of the child his readiness to trust another. Now when we look at youth we find his distinctive characteristic to be his skeptical attitude. Again we do not set boundaries to the period of youth in terms of years. This does not mean that we are blind to biological facts. We simply mean to go by the previously mentioned fact that there is a discrepancy between physical and psychical maturity in the young person. The degree of it varies in differing social environments from place to place in Europe. So we do no more than designate a skeptical attitude as the basic mark of the period in life which we call youth.

Young people express their skeptical attitude quite openly. For example, we note their flouting of the authority of adults, their unmanageable drive for freedom, their ever bolder rejection of folkways—and these are accompanied by an evident feeling of insecurity. In most instances this feeling of insecurity is covered up by bravado in action.

We submit that the skeptical attitude may be a reflection of several facts in the social environment in which our young people live.

The Waning of Parental Authority

In a church meeting a young pastor decided to speak his mind. The attending pastors were older and wiser than he, and also more dignified. He told them, "Today we have to eat the broth that you stewed. Your achievements include the loss of two World Wars.

You helped Hitler to power. Now, in your world of ruins, you clamor for the barracks in which we are to be made what you are." We need not show how shortsighted and naive the speaker was. We want to say that he expressed a feeling that is shared by a sizable portion of our youth.

At the age of ten the young person can already have misgivings about the authority figures around him: parents, teachers, pastors. How does he feel when he sees them do things for which he is taken to task? He notices that parents tell lies. "When the doorbell rings, just say that I'm not at home." He sees that teachers and pastors can be impolite and rude. And he becomes more firmly convinced that adults cannot give satisfactory answers to all questions. It must dawn on him clearly that "all have sinned and fall short of the glory of God." When the adult perceives the ambiguity of existence as St. Paul did, "For I do not do the good I want, but the evil I do not want is what I do," he may manage to go on with it; but the young person is forced to draw revolutionary conclusions from this ambiguity.

The youth is actually forced into the stance of a rebel when in confirmation class the Decalogue is so explained as to make his parents out to be faultless people. This kind of talk sets the stage for a complete collapse of the religious construct in the mind of the young, maturing person. The same result is effected by the make-believe that the parents received only the best of grades in their schooldays. And we attempt to shame our youth by claiming that "such things" as they do were not heard of in our young days. This may indeed be true. But it must also be said that the cultural situation was different. In matters of sex instruction parents and educators are reluctant to tell what needs to be told. This is not Christian. Young people urgently need answers to their questions.

In the secrecy of the young person's heart a change takes place. The repeated failure of adults registers in the child's unconscious mind. There the facts cause childlike trust to wilt and the skeptical attitude to take root. The child becomes the youth. Rarely does the youth rebel openly and tell what goes on in his mind. As a rule he simply knuckles under to the forces that bear down on him. They have him under control at every point of decision-making at

home and in school. In spite of this the youth will, eventually,
come through with a protest. The four-year-old can in all seriousness ask his father to set a ladder on the roof and pick a star out
of the sky. The eight-year-old declares with certainty, "My dad
knows everything." The 11-year-old senses vaguely that grown-ups
really know very little. The 17-year-old is convinced that there is
no greater idiot than his father, or his teacher, or his pastor. Exag-
gerated as this is, it points up the dilemma of youth. This does not
deny that occasionally there is a young person who has kept fully
in touch with life. In youth psychology this posture of protest is
sometimes described as the second negative or contrary period.[4]

The Breakup of Common Morality

When aunt Frieda writes her godchild at confirmation, "Do the
right and fear no one," the pastor must have serious misgivings.
The advice is so shallow. The youth to whom it is addressed takes
note and is sure that it is false. From his experiences with friends
at school he has long since learned that honesty is not upheld as
the best policy. He laughs at mother's claim that she can detect a
lie at the point of a speaker's nose. Youth, like all others, do not
know what is right or wrong unless they learn from the Word of
God day by day.

In the spring of 1949 I noticed a storm signal at the door. Before me stood my confirmand Helga, sobbing. The marks of her
father's hand still showed on her cheek. The words she hurled at
her parents and adults generally cannot be repeated here. The
state of affairs was this. On her way home Helga had come past
a fruit market, stolen victuals, and proudly presented them for the
evening meal. She had done this with the conviction that she would
be commended. Instead, she was beaten by her father, who had
recently returned from a prisoner-of-war camp. Now she was emotionally shocked. She wept, and she cursed and said, "Every morning for two years I had to get up at four o'clock in the morning
and go with Mother and two aunts to the railroad yard. There I
had to crawl under the covering of the sidetracked cars, toss vege-
tables and fuel onto the roadbed. The grown-ups gathered the

stuff up. Each one always rewarded me with fifty pfennigs. Then I was a dear Helga, today I get a beating. What a mean sort these grown-ups are."

Helga was right. We grown-ups are an ignoble lot. Every time adults demand prayer and churchgoing of an adolescent and fail to do so themselves, they widen the rift between youth and adults. The gulf between the generations widens every time parents fail to admit error in order to insist on parental authority. How much better it would be if parents and children would join hands as learners of him who is the Master of all.

Here is a case in point. In confirmation class we were discussing prayer and how prayers are answered. The children had been urged to speak their minds at any time. So Ute did this. She asked a question. "Daddy was a pastor. Every morning we prayed that he would return to us. He was killed in battle. Next door to us live the Muellers, who quit the church, who never pray. Mrs. Mueller used to say to mother, 'I wish the old man would never come back.' But Mueller came home. More than that, every now and then he beats his wife and children so terribly that we have to call the police. Pastor, now tell us, why is this?"

A person trained in theology will probably smile and bring up the old problem of theodicy. But for Ute everything hung in the balance at that moment. Thirty pairs of eyes were trained on me. The silence in the classroom was awesome. Yet this was not a rare experience for a pastor. I went to Ute, a close acquaintance of mine, laid my hands on her shoulders and said, "This I do not know." Immediately breathing was easier in the class. A young voice reassured me in the accents of a Berliner, "It's true, sometimes grown-ups do not know." Not one of us knows. But we opened our Bibles and read the prayer of Jesus in Gethsemane. We settled with the fact that Jesus too was denied answer to prayer. He had to drink that cup. Then we went from Good Friday to Easter and understood that God's way prevails.

Ute's question was not answered, really; but we joined hands and concluded with the hymn, *Weisst du, wieviel Sternlein stehen?* ("Do you know how many stars there are.") The last stanza, *Gott im Himmel hat an allen seine Lust, sein Wohlgefallen, kennt auch dich und hat dich lieb* ("God in heaven has his delight in all of us, is well pleased with us; knows you too, and loves you so") had made us aware of our solidarity as people who are puzzled.

The Fading Away of Fairyland

We have already referred to the fact that stories of the deeds of God are told along with fairy stories. Jesus, Little Red Riding Hood, Hansel and Gretel, are met on the same level by the child. In time the fairy companions of childhood are given up. It has been discovered that they are not true. And so the stories of Jesus also become suspect as to their truth. To be sure, we do see our confirmands pay close attention to accounts in the New Testament. But many times they do this without committing themselves to appropriate response. After confirmation they quit the church. We must grant that some who hardly ever gave satisfactory answers in class join a church-related youth group or put in an occasional appearance at church services. This is a happy experience for us. Rarely is our teaching in confirmation class so impressive that the pupils leave the place in quiet composure. More often they lapse directly into the gibberish of the young.

Why is this? Do we probably have a different person in the pupil than we think? We should understand that when the child eagerly listens to what we teach, he is settling back into the coziness of being a child. Young people generally have an unconscious longing for protected childhood, yes, even for the status of a baby. A whole series of neurotic symptoms indicates this. Bedwetting (enuresis) is one. Another is the rhythmic turning of the head from side to side during sleep *(iactatio capitis)*. A further fact to consider is that a pupil may like to turn to fairyland even though he does not take any of it seriously. It is a fact, then, that our young catechumen is not the person that we like to think he is. The less delicate soul in class makes his defiant protest known to us in a different way. He listens, surmises that the same fairy lore is being presented, and he is done with it. Then he stirs up trouble and makes himself a disciplinary problem. What shall we do?

A confirmation class will have to be conducted differently than a public school class. Also it must be quite unlike mother's fairy tale hour. A few simple techniques may be helpful. For example: Avoid having the pupil rise to recite, let him volunteer what he has to say, and pass it by with a touch of humor when he gets out of line. Above all, be aware of the attitude we mentioned earlier, namely, the solidarity of the puzzled.

To all this must be added that it is necessary to foster sociability. The need for this is greatest in urban areas. A dinner for class members and the pastor at confirmation time will help. The group should be limited to about thirty. A hike with the pastor is good if casual discussion is made a part of it. The pastor may take the class camping for several days. This affords freedom of contact. And it can be made an occasion for conversation on Bible themes in small groups. Some students will feel more free to talk with the pastor while tenting in the night with him, who is as ready to sleep on straw as are the rest. By it all, demonstration should be made of the radical otherness of the Word of God. In the interest of achieving close contact with young people the pastor may invite them to counseling sessions with him. Assurance must, of course, be given that things told will be kept strictly confidential even from the parents. And never, no never, dare there be any leaking of confidential information.

A very excellent way of promoting good fellowship is the liturgical service of prayer and praise in song. This may at first seem strange to youth and be met with reluctance, but it will help to open their souls to the things of God. We shall have more to say later about the liturgy as an aid in the care of souls.

The Loss of Goal-image for Self

The psychologists used to say, "Before every person stands an image of what he wants to become." They meant that a person develops according to the laws of projection, of transference, and of maturity in body and mind. Personal growth also follows the law of impression. The prospective effect of an impression on the development of character may be positive or negative. Imagery has come into play in our day as never before. The means by which an image is made are essentially speech, printed word, picture, and personality. Which one of these will be most impressive for a person depends largely on the mental disposition of the individual. But the picture merits our special attention.

It is an accepted fact that experiences are registered in different layers of the mind. We have the layer of the rational and the layer of imagery. A further layer is hard to define because it is beyond the other two. We could probably speak of this as the layer of "mystical vision." It lies closer to the layer of imagery than to any other function of the brain that we know of. The means of impression that are most prominent among us center in the picture. We have the moving picture, television, and certain forms of juvenile literature (comic books). These definitely have to be taken into account. It is not only the psychological research man who knows this. We all know it. Our speech betrays this by its embroidery of pictures—proof that we register our experiences in the mental layer of imagery. One says, "I was in the picture." Another declares, "The event stands concretely in mind." A third has it, "I could paint a picture of it."

The picture is not a new thing. We may say that every generation has been decisively impressed by pictures. Therefore we now deliberately appraise works of art as to their cultural and psychological significance. Then there is a further fact to be reckoned with. No man can register his impressions on a self-selected layer of his mind to the exclusion of other layers. Pfahler's study *Der Mensch und seine Vergangenheit* (Man and His Past) forbids this notion. Furthermore, if we bear in mind that only the human being produces forms of art just to be producing them, we shall understand that there is a definite relation between primitive pictures preserved in caves and pictures offered in certain smut magazines. Both are eloquent without titles. At this point we must judge these works of art neither as to their historical significance nor as to their moral worth. We are simply making the point that man has a penchant for pictures and that he expresses this penchant according to the milieu and stage of development in which he lives.

Every generation is also impressed by definite ideals. The bearers of these ideals show up as types of some form of living. Our name for these types that characterize certain forms of living and have molding influence is goal-image for self *(Leitbild)*. (We would prefer the Greek word *typos* for type, but this is forestalled by C. G. Jung's preempting of this word for another use.) Our goal-images are not what Jung calls archetypes. His archetype is something like a primitive picture that emerges from the layer of the mind which Jung calls the collective unconscious. Our goal-image is a real type of personality, derived from the past or the present, to which the young person feels attracted and which answers his longing for "what he should become."

At the turn of the century young people had definite goal-images by which to be impressed. The types were of officer, official, commercial magnate, woman teacher, deaconess, and of pastor. These were the types by which the generation that lived from the beginning of the century to the end of World War I was, consciously or unconsciously, impressed. And the types were not mere wish-images—they were realities as tangible for youth as persons can be. Goal-image and example coincided in most instances. In the interest of psychological precision we must distinguish between goal-image and example. An example is always an existing person; a goal-image is very much more. And now, using the sense of *typos* as Jung has it, we may say that the youth's goal-image is strongly influenced by whatever archetypal conceptions he may have.

The generation of World War I had acquaintance with goal-images that had bearing on education for a career as well as with examples of persons who were embodiments of these goal-images. Thus the person born in 1902 had a pretty good idea of what he wanted to become when he had come to the maturing of his sexual functions. The situation was favorable to him. Edward Spanger considers planning for life an important criterion for this very period in life.

Now as to goal-images and our youth. The situation is not so favorable. Goal-images either do not exist at all for our young people, or if they do, they have become suspect in the minds of critically thoughtful youth. One can hardly deny that the prevalence of totalitarianism has caused a decline in the number of personalities who exist as such in the sense of *personare*. Moreover, the personalities that we do have feel themselves to be quite self-sufficient; quite deliberately they do not give credit to the grace of God for what they are. The genuine per-son *(personare!)* is rare. When we do meet with such a personality, he is a big, lonely light shining in the darkness of our personless time. We are reminded of Albert Schweitzer and Dietrich Bonhoeffer.

Since there are no more real goal-images for the young person, and because it has become a question for him whether it is good to live by the ethic of officer, industrial magnate, or official, psychologically speaking, there now is a vacuum; and the pseudo-goal-images of our time rush into the vacuum. We should, therefore, understand why the lad of our day so readily follows the lead given him by the gangster movie, and why the girls tilt their heads and make gestures in imitation of moving picture actresses, not being aware of doing this. Every young life wants to take on character. In view of these facts, we dare not say that films and smut books are quite harmless. Certainly, we cannot support such a claim with the argument that we have always been exposed to that sort of material. In the past there was this difference that the dangerous goal-images were conveyed chiefly by the spoken or written word and found lodgment in the rational layer of the mind and not in the layer of imagery. Besides this, the valid, convincing goal-images were fortified by the presence of numerous personalities in society. Young people were enabled to reject bad goal-images and ignoble personalities. Today the situation is totally different.

We shall later refer to the picture and its uses as an aid in caring for souls. Here we want only to show that false images jeopardize wholesome development of person and character. Our focus is on catechetics and the pastoral care of youth. The evangelical church has a treasure of men and women from which home, school, and church may draw. They became great men and women by the power and grace of God. In each of them, no matter in which of the past two thousand years he or she lived, goal-image and personality merged. If we continue to teach in catechetical class as though there had been no significant men and women between Paul and Luther, and none from Luther to Bonhoeffer, and if we decry all serious concern with the "saints" as Catholic, we only show that we are not responsibly facing up to our task of guiding and impressing youth.[5]

We can also make good use of film, radio, and television as media of proclamation. The rediscovery of the Book of the Acts of the Apostles is on our side. Use can be made of the central concerns of modern art. Biographies and stories of the saints, adequately interpreted in the context of our time, are important tools with which to combat the inflation of false goal-images that have arisen after the failure of secular goal-images. Personality develops only where the goal-image is discerned. The disintegration of goal-images is one of the main reasons for the uncertainty and growing skepticism of our young people.

Encounters During the Years of the Skeptical Attitude

It is a mistake to see only the negative elements in the period that we are now studying. Moreover, since it is our present purpose to make a psychological assessment of this period of life, it is out of order for us to apply moral value judgments of any kind to the behavior of the child or youth. What we see as "negative" is something else to the youth himself and serves a positive purpose for him as he tries to get a grip on life. As he inquires, though skeptically, and as authority figures fade away for him, he is forced to involve himself in new experiences. The biblical saying that a man "leaves his father and mother" now ranges beyond its usual focus on marriage. And separation from authority figures is not so deplorable at all; in fact, it is a necessary turn in life. That is why youth psychology speaks of severing the umbilical cord, meaning that the young must get loose from mother and manage to get along. Educators must support this necessary separation, otherwise youngsters may get the impression that they are rejected. Unless this stride into independence is taken, there can be no planning for life and no finding of self.

ENCOUNTER WITH SELF

The infant first encounters his own body as he discovers fingers, mouth, feet. His next encounter is with materials. The table is found to be hard when he bumps against it. You can look through but not walk through glass. And things that you throw away do not come back of themselves. Later, at school, he meets the world outside the parental home. In about the 14th year this series of childhood encounters has run its course, only to be repeated in an entirely new perspective. And so there is a new acknowledgment of the self.

Traits of behavior at this age are in large measure expressive of conscious or unconscious preoccupation with the self. There is the evident lethargy of the adolescent girl, the slowness of youth in thinking and acting, the absentmindedness of the adolescent for seconds or even minutes while you are speaking to him, and not least the observable lack of concentration in school and at work. Who am I? What am I? What am I good for? These are questions with which youth is preoccupied. He usually answers them as soon as he asks them, reacting either in gross overestimation of himself or in abject mistrust of his own abilities. He can hardly react except in extremes because nobody can show him the middle course, and, for reasons stated earlier, he usually declines the offer of help that adults make.

In every area of their upbringing it becomes clear that those entrusted to us cannot be protected from life's buffeting experiences. We can at best prepare them for their lonely hours and then sustain them with our intercessory prayers. Each person has his own life to live. This bit of biblical anthropology can serve as superscription to youth's self-discovery.

It is only natural that the discovery of self in the area of sex must be a part of general development. The growing boy discovers that he is getting to be a man—the growing girl, a woman. Whether this discovery makes for disturbance or joy, or whether it is accepted as a matter of fact, depends on previous guidance in matters of sex. If this guidance has been lacking altogether, fear can accompany the discovery of self as a sexual being and can cause much distress. That is why it is so true, as we maintained earlier, that conversance with functions of sex must be gained early, no later than the 12th year.

In this meeting of self as a sexual being self-stimulation occurs. It would be wrong to class it as a perversion. Comprehensive studies have been made in recent years on this problem in western lands. They show that 92% of boys and likely 62% of girls compulsively go through a stage of masturbation. What we see here, then, is neither vice nor sin but a biological and psychological stage of development. The danger in masturbation is not its existence but the possibility of its becoming an addiction.[6] Medical findings prove allegations of harm to the body and disturbances of brain function to be without foundation. Also there are no bodily indicators of the practice of masturbation (rings under the eyes, pale complexion). There is slight possibility that masturbation approaching addiction can occasion a passing lack of concentration, because it requires intensive attention to sexual images. Such an overworking of the imagination may sometimes cause light and temporary nervous disturbances in emotionally labile children. Also there is no immediate connection between masturbation in youth and marital impotence. To be sure, a false reaction of the teacher who insists that by "such a thing" the human being will become sick, can later on cause the wife to be frigid and the husband to be impotent.

The young person finds himself bored with life, not pleased with his environment and not satisfied by his social contacts. Yet he has a libidinous yearning, a vital impulse, a craving for enjoyment of life. This is built into him. So, for want of satisfying social acceptance by others, he turns to himself and practices self-love. This is how masturbation comes about. It must be understood in view of the total situation in which the young person lives. The father can be helpful to his son by first ignoring what goes on. Then, he sympathetically confesses that he once went through all this himself. The father will counsel with the boy on the facts of the physical and social situation in which the adolescent child finds himself. Prohibitions and moralizing lectures only drive the child to further depreciation of self and abet his urge to self-stimulation.

From the psychological point of view, meaningful activity, emphasis on developing natural capacities, participation in crafts and sports, are most helpful to the child as he wrestles with his problems. The natural slackening of endeavor in school must not be penalized with denial of joyous activity. This could drive the child to downright perverse activities. The concepts of clean and unclean, chaste and unchaste, cannot be applied to this period of adolescence. The incident of Onan given in the Old Testament has no bearing on our subject either; its pertinence is rather to the prevention of possible conception. A good purpose can be served by appealing to the will and by challenging the person to fight the good fight.[7] The best help is not given by prohibition but by positive guidance, prayer, and the assurance of the presence of God as one participates in the Sacrament.

ENCOUNTER WITH THE SUBSTITUTE FAMILY

At the crest of the crisis in adolescence, youth has, for reasons given above, lost his ties with the family, or has at least loosened them for a time. He cannot, however, live outside all fellowship. So a substitute family is formed. Before the two wars individuals of a kind were put into groups, and these were accepted as the substitute family. But now the group is formed from varying points of view. The selected company is small as a rule. The boy generally has three or four friends of his own age, the girl contents herself with one girl friend. In the summer we see groups of three or four travel on bicycles or buses. The accoutrements of the erstwhile *bündischer* youth, such as pennant and guitar, are not in evidence.

The composition of the groups varies remarkably. Political views are hardly ever involved. It is less by common ideologies that youth get together than by certain ways of behavior peculiar to their character. This is a new fact that has not yet been taken into account sufficiently in a rigid system of grouping young people. In the substitute family all those things are discussed that cannot be talked over with adults who are no longer considered trustworthy. We ought not hinder the formation of these substitute families. We shall also have to accept the fact that conscious homosexual or

Lesbian influences as a rule rarely enter in at this stage of development. At the same time, though, the presence of homosexual groups
of boys cannot be denied. These have been known before. But there
is no evidence from which it can be concluded that the percentage
of homosexual groups of adolescent youth is greater today than it
was previously.

The young person has a way of being highly selective in his
choice of members for his substitute family. His selection, however,
is not made in accordance with the value categories of the adult
world. The touchstone of selection has no connection with the fa-
mous inferiority complex. Selection is made quite wholesomely of
persons who give promise of enhancing one's own development.
After a while the substitute family falls apart rather quickly and
without given reasons. It seems as though the end of a stage of
development were being signaled by a sudden breaking off of
former relationships. In all this we can plainly discern the resump-
tion of the child's line of development: discovery of self, of environment, of materials, accompanied by a general interest in nature
studies and even in problems of the philosophy of nature. The
divine rhythm of life becomes discernible.

ENCOUNTERS WITH THE OPPOSITE SEX

On the day that Hans on his own initiative trims his fingernails
and Erika spends more time than before dressing her hair, alarm
is sounded in the parental home. We have not yet become accustomed to the fact that encounter with the opposite sex cannot be
hindered any more than the cutting of teeth in the infant. This is
not a finding of a materialistic-mechanistic psychology but the
working out of a divinely created rhythm. The fact that human
beings were not created all one sex, but male and female
from the beginning, as the Bible has it, most certainly carries with
it the affirmation of the sexual reality in human life. Androgynous
concepts have come to the fore frequently in the ethics of the
church, but these had as background something other than biblical
truth; they were derived from Greek (Plato) anthropology and
mysticism.[8]

The Bible always views man in polarity with his surroundings and so also posits the tension between the sexes because of their differences. It is in affirmation of these tensions that the existence of the human being is fulfilled. This is not to say that human existence is fulfilled by sexual union. Physical union is indeed essential but by no means the only determinative factor in the sexual relationship. In human relationships the encounter of man with woman in the totality of each allows each to grow toward fulfillment of his distinctive assignment in life.

Our human existence makes for no other possibility but that we meet each other in our sexual peculiarity, be that in school, at work, in public life, or elsewhere. Thus the company of men alone or likewise of women alone must be counted out in what we call "this world." Christ has expressly stated that the problem of sexual tension will be done away only in eternity.[9] It belongs to this life. To set it aside, to render it of no account, to disparage it, or to idolize it is at variance with the creative will of God.

It is not feasible to act as though sexual life should awaken in the moment in which educators think it proper. In human development there is in childhood a period of latent sexual life, but never is there asexual life. The manifestation of it is different in the several stages of development. Since the biologic and psychologic course of development depends neither on the will of the individual nor on the authoritative influence of others, the need for erotic partnership arises as soon as the stage of latent sexuality ends. Unfortunately we have cloaked the erotic in a sultry garb of lewdness. This is an injustice to God's creation. The erotic is the God-willed delight of the one in the being of another. The erotic has a value of its own within Christian ethics and is not attached immediately to the desire to beget. Paul mentions that permanent continence in marriage can lead to unchastity (1 Cor. 7:5). Thereby the Bible softens that frightful word about marital duty and sets it in the light of freedom and grace. The appraisal of any one case must take into account the manner in which the encounter of the respective partners took place in their adolescence. If on principle we burden this encounter with our prohibitions, or if we decry it

under prejudiced suspicion, we share the blame for the atmosphere
of secrecy in which one is prone to transgress the boundary set by
command. The encounter of the sexes must be supported by the
understanding of parents on both sides. From the numerous literary
offerings on the subject we can learn what the possibilities are in
point of method.

Where earnest objection is made to the intermingling of boys
and girls, it is argued that the biologic and psychic development of
the sexes is different both in point of time and in outward expression.[10] While the boy's sexual maturing is connected with extraor-
dinary activity and desire for discovery in every domain, the
girl shows exactly the opposite symptoms. Her outward expression
is her introversion, the creation of a domain of her own, into which
no one, least of all her own parents, may intrude. From these facts
the demand is seriously made that the sexes be separated in school,
in youth movements, and on the street.

In spite of the recognition of the difference in development, we
shall have to maintain that the basic principles of human guidance,
namely the principles of mutual accommodation and habituation,
must not be set aside summarily even in this stage of life. If the
sexes are separated during this significant period of development,
a false partner-image of a positive or negative sort will be formed,
because the possibility for correction through personal contact is
missing. The girl idealizes the boy as she daydreams, and often
unconsciously carries this dream image with her as she enters marriage. This can lead to catastrophe. The boy on his part sees the
girl's course of maturing and has no understanding of it. The girl
who was his playmate (*Spielgefährtin*) yesterday is his spoilsport
(*Spielverderberin*) today, and he thinks her proud and silly. Here is
where the prevalent low regard for woman originates, particularly
in Germany, where to this very day it is noticeable in marriage and
in public life.

We shall, therefore, in deference to both principles, have to steer
a middle course. Evangelical ethics, biblically oriented, cannot
militate against coeducation in school and young people's leagues.
Moreover, it is just as impossible to bring the sexes together in

these areas of life timed exactly with puberty, as is attempted now and then. Separation as well as frequent bringing together in school, congregation, and parental home will be necessary.

Education for marriage is neither a matter of theoretical lectures for the sake of enlightenment nor a matter of arranged trial runs. Preparation for marriage proceeds as does married life itself: One dares to undertake it confidently only by the freedom given through the Gospel. Evangelical ethics can have it no other way.

MAN AND WOMAN

We hold to the proposition that from the beginning of his creation man was not just of one sex. From this fact we derive for evangelical ethics and for psychological method the polarity of mankind. The difference between the two sexes pervades the whole structural and functional situation of man. We therefore have to underscore heavily that the biological difference between man and woman is but one phase of the total difference between them.

Bovet points out that by and large the relationship between the sexes dates back to an original hostility. Zoology shows some parallels. The hamster, for example, kills every female of his species he meets except in the mating season; and there are species of spiders whose females devour the males right after they have mated. We must not draw Darwinian conclusions from this hostility and apply them directly to the tension of polarity that arises between the human sexes.

At his creation man forthwith transcended the biologic-automatic function of sex and proved himself a creature standing apart, whose distinction inheres chiefly in the fact that he is free to sublimate his biological drives into dynamics of the spirit. However, we must keep the lesson of zoology in mind and learn that taking man to be purely a sexual being will lead to a beastly "devouring" of one sex by the other.

Biblical anthropology has it that the structural and functional difference between the sexes is balanced by their equal value. Man and woman are designed for partnership with each other in covenant with God, of which they are capable also after the fall (Gen. 4:25). In contrast to religious myths, in which ideas of an incarnation often turn up as incarnation of divinity in animals, the New Testament has only the incarnation of God in man. It is from this fact that biblical anthropology derives the dignity of man.

Humanity is not dependent upon sexual potency or impotency— it is beyond sexual or constitutional differences and has its peculiar dignity in partnership with God. Where this is no longer held, there man is made out to be less than human (Unmensch).[11] The dignity of the human being thus established has its pertinence precisely at the point in biblical anthropology where we speak of polarity between the sexes, recognize the differences between them, yet hold to the equal value of each person. The basic difference between man and woman pervades every area of life. You see it in gestures, organs of speech, sensitivity, reaction, ability to cope with fate, attitude toward life and death. It is only when a woman is hindered by circumstances from realizing her womanhood and a man is not free to function as a man that the one will simulate the other. In every instance, though, this effort brushes close to neurotic deviation.

In his book on understanding woman (Die verstandene Frau) Eberhard Schaetzing points out how woman exhibits unique approachability and has unique forms of response when she is faced by a man. The pastor should be keenly aware of this—as, indeed, he usually is. Even absolutes (Grössen) like truth and honor become relative in the moment when woman is laid claim to for her womanliness or man for his manliness. Intuition and logic come into play decisively—which, by the way, are patterned differently in woman than in man. C. G. Jung has often used the fact that the heathen religions employ priestesses as exhibit to the point that woman has the greater capacity for sensitive empathy to carry another along with her.

A contemporary poet once declared that he had begun to understand his wife only after their golden wedding, but he had been an open book to his wife at the end of their honeymoon. This humorous statement probably conveys more uncommon sense and psychological insight than most of us want to admit. Every married couple may experience woman's uncanny insight. She cautions her husband about a certain man, failing to give convincing, logical reason for her aversion or suspicion. The husband's reaction then is something like this: "Give me logical proof for your evaluation." She only shrugs her shoulders. He makes light of her opinion. Still he is haunted by the conviction that time and again her views have been proved correct. But since God created human beings to be something other than automatons, the married man will have to use his own wits.

Physical factors in a woman, moreover, condition her psychic life; and psychic factors in her affect her physical life. In any case, man is the aggressive partner—he demands and requires. Woman is the passive partner—she yields, anticipates, and keeps more silent even under pressure of malicious slander. This demonstrates how the psychical and the physical are inextricably interwoven. Since the wholeness of self in both man and woman cannot be broken into soul, spirit, and body, man and woman must meet in the entire being of each. Marriage, then, is the continuous encounter of the whole husband with the whole wife. There is a measure of failure in this encounter from the start, if part of the threefold self is isolated or overemphasized. We join Karl Barth in pointing out that the biblical statement that "they become one flesh" is misunderstood when it is made to refer chiefly to the sexual.[12]

In the same breath we emphasize that a relationship between husband and wife is not possible at all unless the sexual difference between them is noted, reckoned with, and experienced. We want to be wary of mystifying or of disparaging this fact. We affirm it. After puberty man and woman confront each other in the entire manhood and womanhood of each. And our thought is not first of a sexual relationship when we assert that a man becomes a man only by the good offices of a woman, and that a woman experiences and finds herself only in encounter with a man. Because it is "not good that the man should be alone," it is no good ever, on principle, to advocate the separation of the sexes at any time in life.

We have already mentioned that the experience of youth bears this out. Now we widen our scope beyond youth and take marriage as a specific instance of encounter between the sexes, but not as the only possibility for the discovery of self. It is possible for a man to be a total man and for a woman to be a total woman outside of marriage. But the distinctiveness of sex is not achieved when one turns away from or rejects the other.

Since all actions of a man are under creation's law of the wholeness of man, the togetherness of male and female souls is expressed in bodily union, and this bodily union sinks to a bestial level if community of mind and soul is lacking. The New Testament recognizes this relationship between husband and wife in all the intimacy of one toward and with the other; moreover, it uses this as illustration of the relationship between Christ and his church. It behooves us therefore to take seriously the wholeness of the physical relationship between the sexes.[13]

In this frame of reference it devolves upon pastoral psychology to expound and clarify the trichotomous relationship of spirit, soul, and body as the New Testament has it in 1 Thessalonians 5:23. The New Testament has man participate in creation particularly for the preservation of his kind. This is prominently the area in which man is co-worker with God (1 Cor. 3:9) and knows himself called to be God's builder and husbandman. In this area physical relationship for procreative purpose is an act of obedience to a command of God.

Sex as Such

Man and animal are both subject to the will of God by which they are to perpetuate their own kind. For this purpose both are endowed with their strongest drive. Beyond this, man and animal have nothing more in common in the area of sex as such. The comparative working out of the procreative drive gives further proof that man is not just a developed animal but a creature apart.

It is true that procreation accords with the will of God (Gen. 1:28), but it is equally true that for man procreation is not the only purpose that is served in sexual union. This is demonstrated by the fact that man's sexual urge is not rhythmically tied to seasons of the year as is the animal's but is at his disposal at all times.

Man associates a feeling of shame with his sexuality; this means that on the spirit side of himself, he recognizes his genuine humanity. The sexual activity of the human being is always carried out under the signature of shame. When the human being hides himself from God out of shame, the reason for this is not an act of sex but an act of disobedience to God. This fact is usually ignored. When we, then, take the threshold of shame as a necessary phenomenon and posit the dignity of man on it, we expressly point up that, in a given case, this is exactly the opposite of prudery. Sex acts of animals are done with no regard to exposure. The human being, on the contrary, experiences shame when his sex acts are exposed to view; he feels this shame in the degree that he is a human being and has not yet sunk to the animal level.

This observation has weighty pertinence to the question of premarital sexual relationships. We shall have to grant that the New Testament does not give directions in the matter of premarital relationship, nor does it clearly tell under what circumstances or when marriage really begins. But hand in hand with gynecological and neurological experiences of our time we shall have to say no to premarital relationships. We must not let ourselves be dissuaded by the statistics.

The results of research in West Berlin make us face the fact that at the moment a full 40% of our 14- to 16-year-old girls have sexual relationships, some of them quite regularly. According to Kinsey a mere 17% of girls under 25 years of age enter marriage as virgins. These statistics from America would hardly vary much in Germany. It is impossible to determine the number of men who have their first sexual intercourse after marriage; doubtless, though, the number is smaller than that of the girls.

We know from psychiatry and neurology that in rare cases the responsible medical doctor must advise sexual activity in order that functional disturbances of various sorts may be avoided. Even so, two fictions are still held: that masturbation does organic harm, and that continence before marriage causes organic and nervous injury. Every time a girl engages in intercourse before marriage her shame and anxiety become more intense. The unworthiness of the act, the fear of being caught at it, the impossibility, in most instances, of having the emotional experience run its course fully, often make for psychological traumata which cannot be overcome when marital relationships are undertaken.

It is a fact that a large percentage of unhappy marriages stem from a lack of physical satisfaction because the feelings of fear from premarital experiences on the girl's part are carried over into the marriage relationship, and the young wife does not achieve participation freely and fully.

We likewise reject intercourse engaged in for the purpose of making trial of the physical suitability of man and woman to each other. We do this on medical and psychological grounds. Naturally, there will be instances of bodily inadequacies or of disturbances caused by illness which make sexual satisfaction or even procreation impossible. But these can be determined by simple medical examinations before marriage. The concept of trial marriage has no place in human existence. Human life is ventured into—it is not tried and then accepted or rejected. No man can enter a profession by trial in order to determine whether he is suited to be physician, pastor, merchant, or technician. A girl and a boy cannot borrow a child for half a year to find out whether they are suited to be parents. Love, life, and death are taken in stride by trust in God.

It has already become clear from what was said above on the distinctiveness of woman that after sexual intercourse a girl is not the same being that she was before. This holds true as well for her psychological as for her biological self. The responsibility for this change is borne solely by the young man. By his intervention he removes dams and "thresholds," allowing, under contributing circumstances, the girl to sink lower and lower, or at least lays a heavy burden upon her in every instance. The young man may experience release and achievement, but the young girl through this same experience is transposed into oppression and longing. The young man of our day does not know this. He should not be blamed for his ignorance. The blame must rest on parents, teachers, and pastors.

Where a premarital sexual relationship has taken place and actually continues to be practiced, it does not behoove us to berate it unmercifully. We may so state the case after we have made our point of view clear and precise. There are considerations. Among these are the following: inadequate social legislation; the problem of lengthy preparation for an occupation; our false distribution of income by which a man's highest income is reserved for the time of his life when he doesn't need so much any more but lets him be without necessary means when he begins to build his life. These factors are tied in with numerous happenings and conditions whose force is hard to assess. We should therefore not be harsh judges but feel called upon to exercise loving pastoral concern.

Eros

The foregoing exposition clearly allows evangelical ethics to concur with Emil Brunner in his assertion that the erotic has a "right of its own" apart from procreation. Eros and the erotic do not have the same meaning in modern parlance. We should learn from the Greeks that eros is joyous delight of itself. With this as a point of departure we may understand the erotic to be God-willed delight of the one in the "being" of the other. This delight lives above the stuffy lewdness that we meet up with in our "eroticised" public life. We have sunk to the level of the animal. Look at the evidence. There is hardly a toothpaste advertisement or public endorsement of any product but that somehow attempt is made to render it attractive by showing a sparsely clad male or female figure. That is prostitution of the erotic.

We are given leave by 1 Corinthians 7:5 to speak of the erotic in the sense in which evangelical pastoral psychology will have it. Here the Apostle Paul expressly warns against sexual continence that is practiced on principle. Sexual intercourse is here recommended, not for the purpose of begetting children, but "lest Satan tempt you through lack of self-control." This forestalls every perversion and all idolization of the erotic in that Paul (1) advises that the partners in marriage come together, (2) recommends this without reference to begetting children, and (3) brands default in this on principle as unchaste.

In the Old Testament the Song of Solomon is "erotic" in the best sense of the word, as we see it. This remains so even if theology today wants to extend to this book its thesis of the Old Testament's witness to Christ. Likewise 1 Corinthians 13 does not exclude erotic love as such from what we call sex. From this point of vantage we make affirmation of the erotic and put in place of the concept of "marital duty" the concept of "marital delight." A childless marriage is by no means a marriage without purpose. Marital living is commended also out of love and for the satisfaction of both husband and wife. This holds even when there are sufficient reasons why new life can either no longer or ought not to be engendered. To be sure, when a couple weds and is firmly resolved never to "acquire" children, theirs is not marriage before God but sin.

This also clarifies our attitude toward means of contraception in marriage. We endorse the use of them. Responsible action in the deepest sense of responsibility before God includes that a human being have the power of decision as to when and under what conditions he will beget new life. Cooperation in the constructive work of God embraces such responsible action. It must be pointed out, however, that it is not advisable for a couple to begin using means of contraception at the beginning of their marriage, because this would militate against the biological course of the powers of begetting and bearing. Since we are not masters of the rhythm of procreation, it often happens that a young couple who have been using contraceptives for several years of their married life find it difficult or even impossible to effect conception. We must implore our young married couples definitely to want a child at the beginning of their married life; and then, when by the goodness of God they have been given children, they, in responsibility to God, ask the question whether and under what circumstances they should relate their married life to the purpose of begetting children.

To say this does not mean that we are of little faith or that we lack trust in the goodness of God. In every business transaction, in every decision in daily living, in every medical intervention, we let God-given reason play its part alongside the goodness and grace of God. *The Small Catechism* declares that God has given us "reason and all the powers of my soul." This was written by the same Martin Luther who dubbed reason a whore. Thus we can with good

conscience give our affirmation to the erotic and take the consequences of such affirmation.

The question of what contraceptives to use is important. Technical
specifics will have to be determined from case to case in consultation with a medical specialist. Certainly the psychical condition
of the couple will have to be reckoned with when the selection is
made. In passing, it may be pointed out that the "rhythm method,"
so popular today, by which calculation is made of the unfruitful
days of the wife, is not dependable. Each shift in the psychic lability
of the wife, inception of sickness, every sort of excitement and every
biological change, as the years go by, can make for variation in the
so-called unfruitful days. Pertinent and reliable literature should
be available to every pastor.

Redemption of the Erotic

The world in which we live is bearable wherever we experience
it as a redeemed world. Wherever this is not so, the world remains
puzzling and basically senseless. The prevalence of law in the world
does not make for redemption. The same natural law that brings
about the rhythm in the seasons of the years also makes for floods
and avalanches that wreak havoc in creation. No more does the
operation of law in the erotic, whose own lawful operation we have
just now recognized, effect redemption out of its own resources.
Redemption comes about in the relationship of the I to the Thou.
Since one cannot grab himself by the hair and pull himself out of
the mire but in the effort only sink deeper into the morass, there is
no redemption by one's own efforts. Is the erotic in need of redemption at all?

Even as a marriage without the erotic succumbs to weariness, so
the overerotic union founders in loathing. This holds in every area
of the erotic, and so also in the area of the Dionysian-erotic outside
the area of sex. This fact has never been denied by the sex ethics
of mankind. The flight of the overcultivated Greek esthete into
homosexuality was in a large measure flight from the disgust of
oversatiated, purely erotic relationship of the sexes. It would be a

misunderstanding of the psychoanalytical therapy of Sigmund Freud
to assert that this therapy fails to recognize the need for the redemption of the erotic.

Van der Velde's book on technique in marriage goes into every
nice detail but begins and ends with the statement that technically
directed eroticism leads to collapse of genuine sexual relationship.
We must admit, however, that there is a wide difference between
theoretical recognition of this fact and practical conclusions that
may be drawn from it, be that for analytical therapy or for pastoral
care of souls.

The Bible gives us the picture of a fallen creation. It is significant
that in complete misrepresentation of this biblical fact the cause of
the fall is often set forth as the erotic-sexual relationship between
Adam and Eve. But this is not the case. The feeling of shame at the
mutual recognition of nakedness arises (Gen. 3) not as a result of
erotic-sexual encounter but as a result of disobedience to God and
of the consequences thereof. The command of God not to eat
of the tree of knowledge was given, not because of human sexuality,
but to uphold the boundary between divine almightiness and
human pseudo-almightiness. It was transgressed because the human
being always wants to be like God in knowing good and evil.

At this point comes the break between God and man, which the
Bible calls sin. It does not come about by reason of the sexual or
the erotic being of man but by reason of man's transgression of a
boundary set for him, which is the same as to say that man wants
to be a law unto himself rather than to submit to law. Modern man
puts it this way, "I live according to my own laws." From here on
the disintegration of fellowship—of every kind of fellowship—is
inevitable. Adam cannot stand up to the question that God asks
him but lays the blame on his spouse. She likewise dares not admit
her guilt but pushes it onto the serpent, that is, onto the partner of
creation that lives with us in this world.

This is the moment the law of enmity springs up between the
sexes and between mankind and the creature. This gulf, which we
face in every phase of our daily living, is the primordial truth of all
earthly existence. Because this gulf is placed there by God, it can
be bridged only from God's side. Only after the break between

them and God had become evident to Adam and Eve did they recognize the nakedness which previously had been self-evident to them. The fact that the human being wears clothes, aside from other good reasons, is really proof that one can no longer bear the other on basis of sexuality alone. Knowledge of this should shield the erotic from every kind of idolization.

The word *agape*, which, as is well known, the New Testament uses for the concept of love, is not to be found outside the Bible in so complex a form. It embraces in some way whatever is related to love in a much wider sense than we have been accustomed to think. It is a comprehensive and enfolding concept, not a separating one. Love becomes visible only in sacrifice. Love is measured by the lover's readiness to sacrifice. This prevails equally in giving and in withholding for the sake of love. A young woman will definitely gauge the genuineness of a partner's love by the degree in which he is able to make the sacrifice of restraint by the very reason of his love. The erotic at first urges the lover to seek out the beloved in order to gain selfish release. This is not a matter of moralizing judgment but a simple statement of a natural fact. By the *agape* which enfolds the erotic, the I seeks the Thou through self-sacrifice. In this way *agape* redeems the erotic.

It must not be overlooked that in this world there is only one possibility of seeing and grasping the essence of *agape*. This is given in the person of Jesus Christ. Since Good Friday and Easter there literally is no other place where the sense of love can be grasped and structured except at the "place" where the Gospel is proclaimed. This is not to say that sexual liberation and "happy marriage" can be achieved only by human beings of Christian commitment. But it is to say that meaningful living in the polarity of the sexes—to which sexual relationships are of the essence—actually can continue enduringly only where the life and work of Jesus Christ is not ignored.

MAN AS HE AGES

It takes us somewhat by surprise when we notice how much people are occupied in our day with the problems of youth and marriage while the problems of the aging, psychological problems and problems of spiritual care, are slighted. Our inquiry into the psychology of youth runs far ahead of any comparable research in aging. One must be curious about this. Why is it? Certainly, the reason is not that we know so much more about the old than we do about the young. It may rather be that in our basically materialistic era we need the young and can do without the old. Also we are prone to shove out of awareness whatever in our daily living discomfits us, poses difficult questions for us, or makes us think about things that we would rather not have in mind. We actually do have a greater variety of difficulties with older than with younger people; and so we put these very people out of sight and out of mind. Of a piece with this is our practice of hiding the painful concomitants of birth, of decline, and of death. The hiding places are the hospitals and homes for the aged. Seldom are children born at home, and rarely are caskets carried out of the house in which the deceased lived. To state these facts is to criticise our culture.

Since we are so greatly concerned about research in youth, it could seem as though we were making good in our social concerns. The fact is that we are still lagging in them. The touchstone of love for older people shows us to be lagging. Psychological and sociological interest in the aging population is one thing. Loving concern

56

for an aging person is another thing. On this count we of the church must also cast our eyes to the ground in shame. A large percent of our churchgoers and active congregation members are in the period of "the aging man" in their lives.

At what point in a man's life may it be said that he is growing old? It has become a cliché in our day to say that a man is as old as he feels. This says something on the psychological side that is correct; however, on the biological side it is not true that the process of aging moves along with the chronological years. It is known that calcification in the blood vessels may set in soon after birth; and it is this that slows and finally stops circulation of the blood. Were we to represent living and dying, being young and becoming old, on a graph, we would have to draw a circle rather than a straight line, as the psychologist does. He shows that the stance toward life and the reactions to surroundings peculiar to childhood recur in old age. It must be noted, though, that what recurs is a similar symptom and not a comparable inner experience. The inner experience is almost always different in the aged person than it is in the child. Nevertheless, we may say that a mark of a man's aging is his approximation of the symptoms once exhibited in childhood. It is in this frame of reference that the following discourse moves.

Obstinacy in Old Age

Every aged person is apt to be somewhat stubborn on some point and not easily persuaded by logical argument. The outward symptom of a child's negative response turns up again. Grandfather suddenly takes a notion to sit on but one certain chair. The daughter has bought a new dress for grandmother, but, surprisingly and without good reason, the old lady refuses to put it on. In a gathering of gray heads at church a quarrel flares up because one woman thinks that the hostess has given a larger piece of cake to her neighbor.

Instances of this sort could be multiplied. Now, if we were to conclude from these outward symptoms, so like those of the child in his negative periods of life, that the inner occasion for them is the same, and that we can learn from our treating of the child

how to treat the aged, we would take the wrong tack. Whereas
the defiant attitude in the child is a part of his discovering his own
person, the same attitude in the aged results from what has beat
upon him from outside of him and dates from adversity with which
he is all too well acquainted. As his age has increased, he has experienced ever more fully the stark injustice of human existence.
He was able to face up to it so long as his physical powers were
up to it and so long as he was still quite aware of his own personality. But at the juncture in life at which the erstwhile lady
of the house is made to feel that she has become a more or less
expendable grandmother, distance springs up between her and her
children. At this same juncture in life at which the one-time "chief"
realizes that he is nothing more than an unemployed recipient of
annuity and assistance, a gap opens up before him between him
and others. And with their processes of mind slowing down, these
old people are not able to rid themselves of a haunting sense of
separation from other people. Through the years this senior has
been cheated in life time and again. Let this happen once more,
and a feeling of bitterness touching his whole existence may well
up into his consciousness.

He may not be aware of this change in himself. And it may be
occasioned by so small an incident as having been passed by at the
coffee table inadvertently. Again, all through life his good advice
was respected; now nobody takes his counsel seriously. This strikes
him like a rebuff. His store of experience is greater than that of
those about him. Even so, his most earnest proposals are not accepted, and that for good reason. What happens is that he has
derived a fixed pattern of behavior from his lifetime of experience
and he wants to impose it upon others. The imposition is not well
received. To this rejection he reacts, showing the familiar symptoms
of stubbornness.

It is not possible to make a permanent correction of this bent in
the aging person. The best alternative is to provide meaningful
activity for him. This must be gauged to his capacities, but this will
probably never be done as well as it ought to be, not even in a
highly developed welfare state. A child will change, and thus his

show of defiance is but temporary, but for an older person the opposite may hold true. Thus he is a partner in life by whom we can prove our mettle. When the time comes that this proof is not given them, then a judgment is rendered on the genuineness of Christian existence. This applies less to the individual than to the church as a *communio sanctorum,* which fails to prepare the members helpfully to meet such needs. One admonition here to honor the elderly and another there to stand respectfully at the appearance of a gray head are useless palliatives. Younger people will be faced in the right direction if they are made to understand that problems with aged relatives, tensions between them and older persons, are sure to arise when two or more generations live under the same roof. Moreover, younger persons will have to understand that it is part of their education in life to learn to cope with these problems and tensions.

However, this can be validly held only where social conditions are favorable, and there are obvious exceptions. For instance, it obviously is not feasible for a mother of several children living in cramped quarters to continue to cope with the obstinacy of old parents and parents-in-law and still do her duty by her children. Each case must be considered on its own merits. And in this connection, some biblically realistic thinking will have to be done on the concept of neighbor and the nearest neighbor. For only then can right decisions be made with reference to a mother's duty toward child and toward parent. And one may not invoke the authority of "the good old days." Then one decisive factor was not yet known, namely the factor of housing problem, and that makes a difference.

Thus, as the child needs the nearness of mother and eventual separation from her, so the problem with the older generation must, on occasion, be solved by separation. This does not mean that an ethic is given up because of changing circumstances, nor, most certainly, does it mean erasure of what the Old and New Testaments say about honoring the elderly. But it does mean that the difference between the social situation of that day and of today must be recognized and right conclusions be drawn for fitting practice.

Loneliness in Old Age

A definite criterion of the fact that a man is old is his firm feeling that "no one cares about me anymore," that "I am of no use to anyone." Far and wide, this panicky mood, engendered by the feeling of being shut out, is a big problem in our homes for the aged. It must be granted that from his point of view the aging person is right. His usefulness has become rather slight when compared with his former achievements and with the achievements of which he still thinks himself capable. The fact is that, like the child, he is less and less able to evaluate himself critically and to discern his own limitations as age increases. Ever and again we see an energetic, robust older foreman, or a seemingly vital politician of advanced age, or an official employed beyond the year of retirement—they all appear to meet the specifications for their jobs, yet they fail to measure up to the requirements of their positions. The tragedy of this situation is that the nature of the aged person makes him rather unapproachable. A trustworthy younger man is reluctant to call the elder's attention to his limitations. And so a paralyzing feeling of loneliness overtakes the elderly man. Following are some possibilities for real help, which are derived from psychological understanding and motivated by pastoral concern.

As has already been mentioned, every possible means must be employed to provide meaningful activity within the limitations of older people. The form of activity must be selected with a concern for having the persons feel sure that they are still useful. They want to know that for some reason a younger person could not do that same thing. If a group of older women are knitting stockings in overabundance, it would be lovelessness bordering on sadism to tell them that their labors are of no purpose or use. The emphasis must rather be to the effect that they are rendering a service by which younger hands are relieved of a burden. Pastors, administrators of homes, and deaconesses will have to draw on their inventiveness again and again.

Work that is never praised or appreciated makes for depression and not for release. The similarity between the mentality of the child and the aged may be called to mind again at this point. The old person needs to be praised much and reassured often. The reason for this is his disposition to forget while the child remembers. The daughter who is busy with her work can hardly provide a greater joy for her mother than by saying to the mother that the task just finished could not have been performed nearly so well by the daughter herself. In this matter of meaningful work for older persons, we can easily see why it is more difficult for a man than for a woman. By her very nature a woman is far more able to bear loneliness and disappointment than is a man. Moreover, the man has fewer possibilities for practical activity than does the woman. The only formula that applies is that of genuine love by which tireless search is made for sources of joy.

All this must not be taken to mean that we need merely to find a few tricks and with them get the old person to think that he is not so old after all and that his loneliness is not so grievous. His loneliness is not to be denied, and his fear of death becomes greater with each passing day. This is why our central concern of spiritual care commends itself so readily to the aging person, not as a last resort but as a basic and foremost interest. It would be senseless to assume that old people go to church because they have time on their hands and do not know what else to do. There are those who keep themselves enraged over the claim that the church is a company of old people; and they complain to the world that these old people are a kind of malignancy in the church. What balderdash! Segregation has no place in the church, least of all segregation of the generations.

Verily, the church is sustained in this world by the prayers of old men and women. They are receptive to the facts of faith. Let no one equate this receptivity with senility. These elders are receptive because they are mature. They have become mature without being aware of it and without being demonstrative about it. Experience produced their maturity. They have experienced both the beauty and the emptiness of life. Here is where the dignity of old age comes in. If we can help the elderly to understand that they actually do carry the world on their praying hands, we shall have made it possible for them to overcome their loneliness.

Psychology does not play in here in the least, for we are dealing with a deep and ultimate truth. The significance of the cross and resurrection looms large only against the reality of a perishing world. To be sure, this insight of faith is not dependent on the passing of years. But since the aged person is more aware of moving close to the gates of eternity, the mysteries of God have greater impact upon him than upon the younger. We may live as though there were no God; but no one among us can for long live as though there were no death. It follows that the effectiveness with which the evangelical church can minister to old people will depend on how well she proclaims, not only the message of the cross but also the message of Easter.

Longing for Death

In the aged person we meet with a remarkable polarity: he aspires to live and he longs for death. He may be controlled by just one of these attitudes or he may be torn between the two, but in either case there is tension. Aspiring to live, a man is fearful of dying, for he is anxious not to miss out on anything in life. Longing for death stems from a feeling of disgust and of being rejected; in many instances it is a yielding to physical breakdown or a failure of bodily functions. When estimated correctly in the light of the New Testament, longing for death is good. It is foreign to the human being in the earlier decades of his life when he seems to stand at some distance from death; therefore deeper spiritual insights and experiences are foreign to him. We know that Paul had a desire to depart and to be with Christ. We also know that at the same time he held this desire in check out of consideration for the service that he still needed to render the brethren. This was tension, the kind in which the aged person lives, though he may not perceive so clearly as Paul what his situation is.

During the last 50 years a great change has come about in the style of living. Today longing for death is closely tied in with the feeling that one cannot keep pace with affairs in this world. Every one of us has been pained at seeing an old man count on his savings and be utterly unable to grasp the fact that he possesses literally nothing.

And there was the incident of the little old mother who strode into the railroad station in Berlin. She rummaged a worthless 50 mark bill out of her purse, muttering about her sons. The Mission sister on duty in the station listened. The sons had forsaken the family estate in East Prussia, and the confused mother averred that they had come to Berlin simply because they were too lazy to work. She would now have done with the "bums." And, tendering her 50 marks, she asked the sister quickly to buy her a ticket for passage to Koenigsberg. Relatives had already been requested by mail to meet her there on arrival. These instances portray the kind of situation in which some old people find themselves in our day.

At this point let us hark back to what has already been mentioned. Envy and hatred may well up over night in genuinely good old people. Pertinent here also is the tension that springs up between grandchildren and grandparents when the latter see and cannot condone the freedoms granted to the children. "Why, this kind of thing was not heard of when we were young." Such a remark is typical of the older person. He can no longer keep up with current ways of doing things. His standards are out of gear with the rhythms of life that have overtaken him. What are we to do in our concern for such a soul? One thing is imperative. Let him keep company with people of his own age, who think and feel as he does. If this can be done at least once a week, it will be salutary. Then he will be in a more genial atmosphere and be free to scold to his heart's content. Precisely this last is important. In the matter of our central concern, which is spiritual aid, it will be well to consider what has already been set forth on the theme of the dignity of old age.

The Old Person and the New Life

The circle is closing. Having established that behavior patterns of early childhood recur in old age, we can understand why the older person can be intimately attached to the child up to, say, his seventh year. Superficially, one could say that this comes about because grandparents are all goodwill toward the child and say yes and amen to everything. Rather than this, the fact is that child and grandparents, at the beginning and end of life respectively, are so close to each other because they are both close to the mysteries of God. To believe, to trust, to be receptive, and to be quite sure that one's own existence is questionable are by no means merely psychological marks, they are also the criteria of being genuinely human; and in these attitudes there can be confrontation with God. If you have ever observed how great-grandmother tells Bible stories to a great-grandchild, you will know what imponderable yet absolutely factual realities serve as ties between the generations. These realities have no other key than nearness to the Child in the Manger. It is significant that this close tie begins to loosen at the very moment when the child sheds the marks of childhood that we have set forth earlier.

By his awareness of the reality of God in life and in death the old person has the great power by which he can overcome his fears. It is likely that only the old man and the young child do feel deeply what fear is. But certainly also only these two are most keenly aware of the reality of the presence of God in their lives. In the hour of the death of one old man I met with the following. After I had experienced the whole depressing fear of dying on the part of a very old man in two successive visits, I found an altogether changed man in the third visit. As I entered his room he requested his relatives to leave. Then he told me in an even, unemotional tone of voice, "Pastor, since last evening two angels stand beside my bed."

I am ready to admit that when I heard him say this I thought of medical phenomena known to me, of functional disturbances in the brain. He evidently read this from my countenance, for he remarked smilingly, "Now you probably also think me crazy." He had been leader of a division of a sizable technical enterprise, quite well-to-do, and lived under certain familiar tensions in his large relationship. From his night table he took his last will and testament, spoke after me sentence after sentence, figured out complicated percentages, smoothed out grammatical unevennesses, so that my thought of an apoplectic condition or of blood clot on the brain had to vanish completely. After we had prayed together, he said, "Till we meet again, pastor. But not tomorrow morning; for during the night these two (nodding gently toward the end of his bed) will lead me home."

The psychological or medical factors in this situation just do not interest us. The decisive thing is that in an encounter with the dying the hidden truth and power of God can become more visible than in any other contact with people.

MAN AND SICKNESS

Sickness is a part of life in this world. It is just as much a primordial phenomenon of our existence as are fear, sin, and the instinctual drives. Sickness brands our situation. Of the numerous phenomena that determine our existence, some move at a tangent to others, some overlap others, and now and then there is even a congruence of differing phenomena. Thus it naturally happens that there is partly slight, partly extraordinarily close connection between sickness and guilt, between sickness and fear, between sickness and aggression. Since God works "in all and through all," the primeval connection (*Urbeziehung*) of all sickness is that between it and God's Word. It is only from this point of vantage that the nature (*Wesen*) of sickness can be plumbed to its depth. This proposition, however, leaves the way open to a dangerous oversimplification of the problem of sickness on the part of a nonmedical person. It may also falsely pit the medical practitioner against theology, particularly against biblical ethics. Clarification of this may be best accomplished by a negative illustration:

For example, when we speak of the relationship between sickness and guilt, we must emphatically reject the moralistic assertion by which, in every case, sickness is interpreted as God's punishment for man's wrong ethical decisions. This holds for the whole range of sickness, even also for venereal diseases—and this needs to be declared emphatically in a book of theology. Since experience shows that some moral aberrations do not result in venereal infection, it cannot be concluded offhand that venereal disease is a priori "proof" of God's punishment. Here much harm is done in pastoral practice. This is true not only because the pastor lacks the necessary biological knowledge, but because this is basically the result of false theology touching the Second and First Articles of the Creed. On the other hand, it cannot be denied that God has some purpose in every instance of sickness. In spite of the uncounted cases of illness that seem so meaningless and terrible, there is, after all, no such thing as the utter meaninglessness of being ill or of suffering pain. However, a linking together of sickness and punishment that allows for no exception is theologically false. It may easily happen that a person, in his relationship to God, may experience the gracious visitation of God in his sickness.

This is not the only point of view from which the sickness-guilt problem may be seen. In the practice of minister and physician the whole complex of questions takes on urgency particularly where the socially deviant behavior of the human being has to be appraised by the question of guilt *or* sickness. At the moment, interpretations are in a whirl. In the first place, we must recognize that socially deviant behavior is farther removed from a person's willful decision than we have been assuming. This is so particularly in the area of sexual perversion. Right now many European lands are attempting to reform penal law with reference to homosexuality.

An inquiry among German chairs of psychiatry disclosed that the responsible university teachers—so far as I have been able to find out—have without exception expressed themselves in favor of repealing public law number 175 in its present form. A simple ethical judgment on homosexuality does not always take into consideration that the whole question is extremely involved and complex. There is no comparison of moral conduct between the culprit of a man who under threat of force or with enticing promises lures a little boy to himself in order to violate him, and a so-called homosexual "marriage" of two mature men through decades. The manifold possibilities for homosexual development, resulting from bad upbringing, stunted social environment, organic incapacities, and physical deformities that repel a partner of the opposite sex, forbid that the homosexual be made an outcast forthwith. Moreover, we may well allow that there is a margin of difference between

the biblical judgment on the "violator of a boy" and the curve of
variation in general homosexual behavior which we have described.
It is to be feared that the false appraisal of onanism as of the Old
Testament character of Onan (who, by the way, did not really
practice onanism) has had its parallel effect in shaping the general
and prejudicial appraisal of the whole concept of homosexuality.
Or again, it is to be feared that this judgment has been formed after
Paul's allegations concerning sexual aberrations in the criminal
quarters of the harbor city of Corinth. In the spring of 1955 the
Anglican Church set up a research board, made up of physicians,
psychologists, and pastors, to express itself, under guidance of the
Bible, as to a new orientation in the area of homosexuality. Similar
efforts are known to have been made in the Scandinavian lands and
in Holland. In Germany work has also been done on this extraordinarily difficult and many-faceted problem.

The laws which have prevailed till now with reference to the
problems of sexual perversion are also no longer tenable. Does it
make sense that through the years homosexual practices of females
go unpunished while the basically similar practices of males make
the man liable to do time in a penal institution? The juridical rejoinder that the male perversion is much more dynamic and therefore ever so much more evident to the public is an argument that
is not true and not convincing. We shall increasingly have to view
perversion as illness and treat it with the means that are at our
command, both medical and pastoral. But this fact does not suffice
to assign perversion to criminality and to make it punishable.

Now that we have already set forth the psychological facts, we
will also have to make the clear statement about the problem of
sickness-guilt that the bane of psychologizing all life situations
enters exactly at the point where personal responsibility with its
consequent guilt is eliminated for psychological reasons. At this
point psychology becomes a modern substitute for redemption,
when it proclaims a message that is superlatively welcome because
it states that in the end man is not to be held responsible for any
of his acts. When all culpable behavior of man is quickly laid to
outside factors such as faulty upbringing, environmental conditions,
hereditary inclinations or biological defects, man is deprived of the

distinguishing acknowledgment that sets him apart from the animals, namely the acknowledgment of his guilt.

In order to set the whole matter into the right light, it seems proper to make an example of the relationship between disturbances in circulation and blamable human conduct. When the heart is damaged because a man has long since forgotten about moderation, his sickness and the resultant dislocations in his family point to genuine guilt that dare not be denied. It is the unrefuted claim of modern medical therapy that no medical treatment can effect a basic cure for the managerial-sickness of our time. In order that a man may properly stride along with the rhythm of living and enjoy the consequent blessing of bodily health, he must meet the conditions of keeping himself within the limitations God has set upon his capacities for work. Here, then, is an instance by which it can become clear what we mean when we speak of the relationship between sickness and guilt. The adjustment of the self to human capacities is firmly tied to the serious reckoning with the reality of death, which many people nowadays no longer find bearable.

In contrast to Hellenism of both the older and newer variety, the Christian faith knows no diminution by death. But death is equally a reality of the perishableness of man and of the indestructibility of God's love. When death is no longer faced as an event of sheer dread but rather as the gateway to the Father, then the prevalent tensions in life today will subside.

Our "therapy in pastoral care" for the sick will thus be under control of the three basic presuppositions on which we have based our exposition. They are: The primordial phenomenon of sickness as being integral to our existence while we live in this eon; the correctly viewed relationship between sickness and guilt; the attitude toward death which holds that it is the gateway to the Father in Jesus Christ.

Visiting the Sick

Preparation must be made for every pastoral activity. This applies especially to visiting the sick. The spiritual side of the preparation is quite obvious. In the long run, visiting the sick can be fully effective only when the sick person is regularly named in the intercessory prayers of the visitor. It is one of the mysteries of inter-cessory prayer that persons who pray for each other, or who know themselves to be borne on the prayers of the other, mutually sense this fact. Primary and basic to preparation is the knowledge of the situation of the sick person, of the condition of his body and of his soul, of his difficulties at home, and of the problems which particularly agonize him in his situation (loss of job, disability, or such).

Wherever possible, inquiry concerning the patient should be made of either his nearest relative or of his physician in order to determine the most suitable length of the visit. In the case of the critically ill this is most necessary. When a morphine injection is phasing out, the patient's pains make him unapproachable. Our visit will not help him but only burden him physically and psychically. If we come to a patient at the same time that his relatives are with him, we can, under certain circumstances, become involved in family tensions, by which any further visit could be made difficult. Naturally, it will not always be possible, whatever the reasons, to make preliminary inquiries. There will also be cases when they are not even advisable. But as a rule, they ought not to be skipped.

One should know before every visit to a hospital or a home what one wants to achieve. Our visits often fail because we have not thought this out beforehand. Not every visit to the sick can have the same purpose. We can hardly tie ourselves to a pattern by which we use Scripture reading and prayer with every sick person no matter what the circumstances. Most certainly, our apostolic service must be in evidence at every visit. But many times it will be necessary to make this evident in an incidental way, perhaps by a single pertinent phrase. A dedicated Christian surgeon spoke to his patient on the eve of his operation about necessary matters. The patient had no churchly connections nor any ties of faith. He tried to tease the surgeon, who was known to be outstandingly conscientious, by saying, "If you make a mistake, matters won't be any worse; then all will be over with, and I will have my rest." The doctor answered, "Are you quite sure of that?" Two days after the operation this patient urgently requested to see the doctor. He began to talk with him about that casual question; an earnest conversation developed, and it gave this patient his first turn toward

Christ. In this conversation this doctor demonstrated that we pastors have something to learn as we deal with people who are strangers to the church.

Since in many instances the presence of the pastor at the sick-bed does not set the patient at ease but rather tends to distress him, overly strong spiritual demands should be avoided. The situation changes at the moment when the sick person gives the slightest hint by question or remark that he craves an answer to the questions forming in the depths of his fears. Precisely these shy but downright serious attempts to form a relationship with spiritual things must promptly register with the pastor and be answered by him.

In the chapter of this book that treats of counseling there is further development of this theme. In general it will be necessary to be as careful and modest in giving answers in matters of faith as the patient is in asking the questions. Things of faith administered in doses that are too strong will prove to be deadly in most cases.

Since there is no fixed pattern for visits to the sick, even as there is none for social services generally, it must also be said that we dare not be too hesitant about the message that we bear. This happened to a pastor who had twice visited a ward and then received letters from the patients which requested him not to return. These people were of the opinion that they did not need a pastor who would entertain them with drivel about the weather or to put forth a commentary on the course of a sickness. They had been disappointed in the young minister for having failed to say anything about God on two visits.

Our experience is that the sick person craves a clear evangelical message at such specific times of his illness as at the start of a new method of treatment, or before an operation, or before release from the hospital, or when his condition changes. For him a fitting word of Scripture without comment will serve well. It is also possible to conclude an otherwise mundane conversation successfully by having the minister lay his hand on the patient's hand and look him steadily in the eye and say, "Anyhow, Mr. Mueller, you still know that it says in the Bible, 'Even though I walk through the valley of the shadow of death, I fear no evil; for thou art with me; thy rod and thy staff, they comfort me.'"

The use of the hymnbook is strongly recommended in visiting the sick. By and large, it is a fact that the man who is estranged from church has a larger store of hymn stanzas in mind than Bible verses. In hours like these the hymn shows itself for what it really is, namely prayer.

The relationship between physician, nurse, and pastor is very pertinent to spiritual care of the sick. In general, and in comparison with other countries, hardly anything has come to pass in Germany on this score. The difficulty of achieving mutual acceptance inheres in great part in the fact that doctor and pastor may indeed be recognizing ever more the close relationship that exists between their respective callings, but each often lacks requisite insight into the particular mission of the other. For this reason they do not achieve fruitful cooperation. Specific proposals and possibilities are to be set forth at another place in this book. Here let it be stated that the whole matter does not turn on the proposition that doctor and pastor should think that both are working at the same assignment. *The proper doctor is concerned only with restoration* (HEIL-UNG), *the proper pastor is concerned only with salvation* (HEIL). For various reasons, the mixing of these two spheres is dangerous for both parties and unbearable for the sick. Medical, psychotherapeutic treatment of the human being and pastoral care do, of course, touch at points and occasionally overlap, but in reality they are concerns that are distinct from each other.

The recognition of this fact does not mean that the pastor should be ignorant of basics in medical and especially in psychological treatment, or that the doctor should think that the work of the pastor at his patient's bedside is of no consequence. Between hospital chaplains and doctors in the same hospital there should by all means be regular conferences and exchange of observations on patients. In most of the hospitals of Scandinavia and Holland this is done. In Germany at the moment this practice is only beginning.

It is certain that we have the same Word of God to speak to both the well and the ill. But never can we use the same method of approach to the sick as to the healthy. A far different manner of address must be made to the depressed patient than, for instance, to the patient who is given to an addiction. To growl reprimands at the bedside is out of order in every case of spiritual care. The concepts of Satan, sin, condemnation, and descriptions of eschatological events are dangerous. Precisely because these are realities and because sickness is a condition of fallen creation, as we have spoken of it earlier, we shall have to be cautious; otherwise we run the risk of encountering forces and powers that we cannot control by human effort. If we are to take seriously what the Bible says about the powers of evil and their connection with sickness, sin, and death, we will avoid making calculated recitals of them at the sickbed.

Now to a special problem. To what extent is a doctor justified or even obligated to disclose to the pastor the status of the patient's sickness? If pastoral care is to proceed relevantly and in depth, the pastor must be aware of the patient's condition. Even so, the situation in Germany is still such that an official request in this regard cannot be directed to the medical association by the leaders of the church. This is a harsh judgment. That this is so naturally does not date from the person of the pastor, nor from his lack of qualification for his work, but it dates from his lack of knowledge in matters medical and psychological. Our pastoral care of the sick will have to continue piecemeal for the reason that the doctor, who has the best of intentions, often cannot responsibly confide his diagnosis and prognosis to the pastor. Directly, this poses for the pastor the problem of truthfulness at the bedside. And this falls upon him with greater urgency than it does upon the doctor. Indeed, for the moment, the situation is made easier for the pastor than for the doctor, because the pastor can usually answer the specific question of the patient with a good conscience and say that he is not informed about the patient's sickness. This fact is the strongest argument that is advanced for letting the relationship of doctor and pastor remain as it now is. But, after all, is this not dishonorable and, at bottom, cowardly? For the Christian, truth is not embodied in a thing, nor in an idea, but in Jesus Christ.

On his rounds of service the pastor is not the slave of a philosophical abstraction nor of a truth that can be rationally grasped; the pastor is the servant of *him* who did not say of himself that he *proclaims* the truth, but that he *is* the truth. It should now be clear that there is no absolute concept of truth. In evangelical ethics the concept of truth is always correlated with the concept of love. The controlling factor of the New Testament is not Platonic truth but *agape*. Thus we can take our stand beyond rigid patterns, beyond medical and theological insistence on what is right. We can let a decisive light fall on the problem of truth at the sickbed. Discussions of the problem we have had to the point of vexation. Love is the thing—not sentimental, civilian love, but love as of the New Testament. And this love has no truck with tactlessness or rudeness.

Then comes the question of whether and how much the sick person may be told of the "truth." This hard question hinges on two premises. First, human beings can never be sure that a patient's condition is hopeless, nor that his recovery is certain. Pastors and doctors both know that the issue is not in their hands. No one knows so well as a doctor what a surprising change may take place even when medical prognosis has pointed to but one outcome.

Secondly, there is difference between patients. One may be an inwardly mature grandfather who means to set his affairs in order before his demise and in that interest calmly asks the pastor how critical his illness is. Another may be a businessman of the same advanced age, interest, and disposition. How different, though, when the patient is only 25 years old and asks the question. Again it is one thing when your patient feels his strength ebbing out after a long siege of illness and has prepared himself for death, and it is quite another thing when a man with a severely damaged heart, who in the slightest excitement may suffer occlusion and death, asks the question of truth concerning his condition. The pastor has to make the decisions, hard as they are to make. In the last analysis, he makes them before God. In any case, and out of pastoral responsibility, he must first consult with the doctor and the relatives of the patient before he answers the patient's crucial questions. Rules are of no use. Rigid patterns of procedure are also useless. This remains: The love of Christ constrains us.

PART II

*Nature
and Method
of Our Proclamation*

COUNSELING

Only man has language as a medium for the exchange of thoughts and for the understanding of one by the other. What this sentence says is not so self-evident as it may seem at first glance. You see, a human being is not limited to a relationship with his own kind. It is possible for him to relate himself to the whole realm of creation. There are human relationships to inanimate objects, to animals, and to the world of plants. In a genuine relationship there is always a transaction. We cannot say that this transaction is possible only between human beings. Man may become involved with inanimate objects (preeminently with objects of art), with animals, and with plants. In our frame of reference, an encounter with anything can be of negative or of positive value. A child's first meeting with an animal may happen in such a manner as to influence the relationship of this child, and of the later adult, to the whole animal world. The same is true of a first meeting with an inanimate object or a plant. However, we must grant that the pedagogical way in which these encounters take place will help to shape resultant relationships. Incidentally, this suggests a question that would merit earnest psychological inquiry: To what extent can release or even healing be effected in a man by his encounter with creation apart from relationships to fellowmen?

Our concern here does not center in man's interchange with creation in general but in the encounter of man with man in the counseling relationship. Strictly speaking, counseling is possible only between human beings. Indeed, lifeless things can be meaningful to us, but they cannot converse with us. Again, an animal has various ways of expressing its feeling to us; but if we think that man and animal can go so far as to counsel with each other, then we humanize the animal in a way that contradicts the sense of creation. This we must not allow. In counseling there is exchange, and there is meeting of two human beings in a relationship touching soul and spirit.

The fact that man can engage in a dialogue bespeaks his dignity. Only when man understands the possibility of his being received into a relationship with his fellowman, and understands this against the background of his position in the whole realm of creation, can genuine counseling take place. Where this is not the case, there can at best be address, exchange of opinions, or discussion.[1] The difference between these and dialogue as avenues for human understanding inheres in the fact that only in dialogue does a man earnestly acknowledge a fellowman to be his God-given partner in all phases of life and take him seriously enough to listen to him.

In address you make your own opinion known for the purpose of convincing, guiding, and naturally also of helping. In an exchange of thoughts the subjective experiences of one partner are set over against the likewise subjective experiences of the other. This is much like trading postage stamps. Finally, there is discussion. What goes on in it, in the last analysis, is pointed up by the root of this Latin word: there is dissection and disjoining of the other fellow's opinion. That is why discussion always hovers close to that frightful word *Auseinandersetzung* (altercation). The sense of the word points up plainly the danger that is a human possibility in person-to-person encounter that is not counseling. It is only in dialogue that the other is genuinely taken as the brother who has God as his Father as I have. Dialogue is at its best when the one is ready to listen to the other, to learn from him, and when this readiness is mutual. We must admit that, by and large, genuine dialogue is but seldom achieved in our relationship to fellowmen.

At the same time that we sing the praises of dialogue as the most excellent way for two human beings to enter into spiritual communication with each other we are in danger of idealizing it and of veering off into reverie. Every counseling session is a meeting of two human beings who are equally involved in fallen creation. Intrinsically, therefore, truly "open counseling" can never be. This must be kept in mind from the start of an effort in pastoral care, otherwise there is a danger of falling victim to idealizing. Involvement in daily frustrations can then threaten to push both pastor and parishioner to the brink of despair. Every counseling session takes its light from the first in Genesis, between God and Adam. Like there, so here; counseling does not begin with a question that man asks, but with the question that God addresses to man. Whether the person is aware of this at the moment, acknowledges or denies it, is not important for a recognition of the nature of counseling. Man's every expression of life, including his speech, is simply an answer to an unceasing question put to him by God. Every reaction of man to God's question is like that of Adam in the counseling session of Genesis 3:9: Man hides when the Counselor speaks to him.

The pastor must know that the person who comes to him for counseling cannot do anything other than hide from whatever the pastor will say or ask. Whoever realizes this will set all moralizing value judgments aside from the start. To begin with, the objective in counseling is not to make value judgments but to listen. The modern trees behind which the participants, including the pastor, conceal themselves in every case are sundry. Temperament, milieu, philosophy, real or imagined sickness, change of feeling, or—and this for sure not the last—our own piety can be the trees behind which we hide to shield ourselves against the challenge of God. Rousseau had something similar in mind when he called out to the students at Geneva: *A bas les masques!* "Off with the masks." Every human fellowship is behind masks. The same is true of the two who meet face to face in counseling. They approach each other behind masks. Thus the counselor must strive to get the counselee to be ready to take off more and more of his mask.

The method of pastoral counseling, not its content, consists in helping the counselee to be as he is and to say what he would like to say. Along with psychological method, the telling means in this effort should be love and patience. Let it be said that in some few cases it may prove necessary, for the sake of love, to pull the mask off with one full sweep. This may, for instance, be necessary when a very conscious striving to be pious stands in the way of genuine counseling and makes spiritual healing impossible.

Three lines of endeavor should be set forth as the directions which counseling must take: *Counseling is loving service. Counseling is release. Counseling is guidance.*

It is important to see these three lines as parallel. This means that service to another cannot exclude his release, nor can there be release by counseling without guidance. Helpful counseling endeavors to follow all three lines. Because of a pastor's constant shortage of time, it is necessary to note that counseling is not a one-time meeting. Thus it may be appropriate, from time to time, to let the counselee know about each of the three parallel interests. No attempt should be made to have them follow in a certain sequence. In fact, a separation of the first two is hardly possible. The service of listening alone makes for release in many instances.

It happens frequently that when the visitor has delivered himself of a practically uninterrupted hour-long outpouring of speech, he suddenly rises, thanks the pastor profusely, and feels eased, even though the counselor has not given a single word of guidance. In such a situation we dare not force further counseling upon him at that time. On the other hand, it would be responsible action only in the rarest cases to discharge him at this point. One should rather take pencil and datebook in hand, invite him to a second appointment, and urge him to keep it.

To have characterized counseling to this extent already indicates the distinctive difference between it and confession. It will hardly be disputed that the practice of confession has fallen away in the evangelical church because the pastor is scarcely aware of the basic methodological, psychological, and, above all, the theological difference between counseling and confession. The meeting of the Lord with Nicodemus in the night was counseling; the meeting between Saul and Ananias was to them respectively confession and absolution.

Counseling is always marked by continuation. The mark of confession is that it brings something to a conclusion for good and for always. Counseling involves the guidance and advice of the pastor;

confession hinges solely on the forgiveness of God proclaimed to the confessant. Pastoral counseling will be preparation for confession in most cases, at least in the Lutheran Church. But to equate pastoral counseling and confession, as this is being done so widely in evangelical pastoral care, fails to do justice to the nature of confession and to the pastoral care of the confessant, and especially to the royal gift of God's forgiveness.

Helpful service always begins with listening. It is characteristic of our time that hardly anyone has command of this skill. But it is a judgment upon us that we do not even try to learn it. It is reported of an American psychiatrist that he, with stopwatch in hand, visited about a hundred Protestant clergymen, and began to recite to each of them about his "own" troubled marriage. At the moment that he was interrupted by the pastor he stopped his watch. In no case did he clock more than 2½ minutes. We should not become excited so much over the method this psychiatrist used as to concede how hard it is for us to do nothing else for 30 or 40 minutes than listen.

We must make the point that this compulsion of the pastor is not to be laid to lack of love or to nervous restlessness. It is precisely the dedicated pastor who often is so charged with his task of bestowing the riches of the Gospel upon a seeking brother that he cannot wait out the time to make the bestowal. But certainly there is another cause: The devilish routine of pastoral practice so often puts the fitting answer for the presented "case" into the mouth so promptly. When we have heard our visitor's first five sentences, we think that we know his whole case and that, naturally, we have the solution to his problem in readiness. In the back of our minds may also be the thought that maybe we can spare the counselee further baring of his soul. This is wrong. What the young medical student learns from the example of his professor and what is an absolute necessity for him when he takes up the often very involved case history which has been obtained from the patient with exacting effort, this the pastor lacks: the conviction that there are no patterned "cases." Every little detail in the case history of the patient is significant. This is true especially for all pathological symptoms. And precisely because neurology and psychiatry are the areas of medicine which are closest to pastoral care, we as pastors have most to learn from them.

One of the daily causes of distress for the pastor is the plain fact that the number of people who come to him for counseling in matters that are purely material or that pertain to outward affairs is far greater than the number of people who come with spiritual concerns and speak of them directly. From this fact the conclusion is generally drawn that the counselee really looks upon the pastor as a kind of social welfare expediter. Too quickly this makes for bitterness and a feeling of loneliness on the part of the counselor. He is then apt to take an unkindly attitude toward visitors and to make unkind remarks about them. The pastor and the teacher, likely also the practicing physician in many cases, too seldom make it clear to themselves that the real concerns of the callers are not openly stated but are covered up by inquiry about practical concerns that are more easily broached.

Here again it is not the evil will or a kind of dishonorableness that prompts visitors to do this. Theirs is an understandable shyness in setting forth the real reasons for their personal failures. Or it may be that the counselee is utterly unaware of the reason for his unease, whether from a psychological or physical point of view. This is what calls for release by counseling. We must learn to discern the soul-situation of the partner as it is hidden behind the scenes. Behind the asking for a pair of shoes or clothing may be hidden the need for more effective managing of the grocery allowance or of the husband's salary. And behind this, again, may stand the real disorder of the person, estrangement from God. Behind the request to be drawn into some work in the congregation, to be visited, or to have a welfare worker sent out to arrange some financial support of the household, there can lurk a screaming loneliness, or marital trouble, or even the very lack of a desire to live at all. Behind the request that a son or daughter be sharply reproved there is, in too many instances, the acknowledgment of failure in rearing them, utter helplessness, or even the hidden, unconscious hatred of a possibly illegitimate child.

It will thus be required in many instances to ferret out what is behind what has been set in the foreground, what is behind the often gruff, saucy demands that are being made. Here, moreover, is the point of departure at which knowledge of depth psychology is just as indispensable for the pastor as it is for the teacher and the physician. What is needed is sober, clear knowledge of a good, psychologically correct technique of interviewing and counseling, so that progress may be made as soon as possible from incidental, superficial things to the real but hidden factor in the failure in life, yes even to sin and guilt.

Unavoidably the counselor will have to inquire about details. This is dangerous to do. Pastoral care can so easily be confused with spying on the soul. Whenever the counselee suspects curiosity on the part of the counselor, he clamps shut. But when earnest concern, above all, when sympathetic love goes out to him, he begins to open up. In the current practice of pastoral care we shall have to muster our courage and ask more detailed questions. These are not just to inform the counselor. Information is needed so that guidance may be given, but the real purpose of asking for details is to bring about release for the counselee. The outcome may be a calmer, more factual consideration of the involvements in facing up to spouse, child, tenant, or supervisor on the job when the details are displayed.

When a woman tells us that she has difficulties in marriage, that her husband is not faithful to her or that he is cruel to her, this can in no case suffice for pastoral guidance. Every one of these assertions is so subjectively weighted and vague and it does not disclose the counselee's own attitude toward marriage. At this juncture we must dare to ask further and detailed questions in the whole area of married life. They are patently in order, even necessary. At this point it is our duty to be sufficiently well informed and oriented in this phase of life that we may be able to give adequately helpful advice.

When a boil is opened and pus comes out, the patient immediately has a pleasant feeling of release and ease. Although the core of the boil has not yet been removed, he will feel that he has already been cured, and he cannot understand why the doctor wants to put him through the painful procedure of getting at the root of the matter.

A similar thing happens in pastoral counseling, for here too release is achieved with accompanying pain. That is why it is urgently prescribed that the whole case positively be not dispatched in *one* sitting.

Moreover, we shall have to expect that something will happen in a genuine pastoral counseling session. Psychology speaks of the problem of transference. This is sure to happen also in a pastoral counseling relationship. A connection springs up between pastor and parishioner. The theory of pastoral practice usually points out quickly that the parishioner is not to be led to the pastor but to Christ. This is correct but can be dangerous. Specifically, this becomes dangerous and loveless when the pastor is not ready to assume the trust, the affection, or even the human love that his parishioner carries over to him. The way to Jesus Christ always goes "through" (in the real sense of the word) a brother. Even as analytical counseling, to be dealt with later, must go through the stages of mistrust, affection, love, and hatred as between therapist and patient, so the pastor should know that in counseling with his parishioner the latter will have to go through these selfsame stages. Whoever does not want this or is afraid of it ought not to be a practicing pastor. Service in this area can burden body, soul, and spirit of both partners. That is also why they require joint prayer, but on the first leg of the way it had better be prayer for each other, praying that the body, soul, and spirit of each "remain unblamable."

Pastoral care is always the giving of oneself. Always, therefore, it involves risk. The whole range of human moods is hurled at the pastor with an intensity that veritably is consuming. At this he should not be surprised or frightened, but he should persevere in it to the end that he may place his ward in the hands of the crucified and risen Lord. Whoever rebuffs the passionate reaction of the counselee by pointing prematurely to Jesus Christ is not engaging in christological soul-care but is simply hiding his fear and lack of courage behind the Lord. But he who goes with the child-in-care over the heights and into the depths of human relationships and leads him in faithful confidence and frees and admonishes him, has

the promise of seeing the countenance of the Lord standing beside
this child-in-care.

Counseling purposely culminates in guidance. In our contemporary evangelical theology we have had more than enough talk on the
theme that there is no formula for gaining a mastery of life. This
contention is right and must not be given up; but it becomes wrong,
and leads to despair, if from this point we dare no longer give
guidance. To be sure, the directive of the pastor must be kept as
distinct and separate from divine command today as the Apostle
Paul kept them constantly separate for his congregation in Corinth
(compare 1 Corinthians 7:10 with 7:25).

It has been a boon for the evangelical church in Germany to have
discovered anew what it means to be a brother. At the same time,
however, we stand in danger of losing the courage that we should
have when we face the fact that we need and must be spiritual
fathers. In England I was repeatedly stirred by the young Anglican
priest's conviction that it is his assignment to be a father to his
congregation. I was similarly moved at seeing how older and mature
people addressed their pastor "my father" quite naturally and were
aware of what they were saying. In our church we have become
brothers and sisters so much that far and wide we do not dare to
be fathers.

Guidance, we know, is coupled with authority. But there is true
authority, and there is something else. Tyranny, holding the leash,
acting as a controlling all-wise force is that something else. Opposites exclude each other. It isn't the father's first duty to gauge
and to judge; the father renders his service when he loves and
guides. In caring for souls it is quite the same. Our first task is not
to evaluate the disposition or deed by a definite category of values
and immediately brand it as positive or negative. Our task is to
listen, to understand, and to heal. Very likely there is a basic difference here between the psychotherapist and the pastor. The doctor
must have an eye for the illness, the pastor is confronted with the
problem of sickness *or* guilt—sickness *and* guilt. The doctor does
not need to train the spotlight of God's Word upon the bearing of
the patient, the pastor must. When God's Word is applied in dead

earnest, then human judging and common moralizing are set aside; and the child-in-care, with all his life, is placed before him who judges by other than human standards.

So we state again the necessity of having the pastor give advice and guidance to his child-in-care. He owes it. Always, though, the counsel must be given with reference to the person's condition at the moment. You do not say to a man who has never swum a stroke, "Now you've got to swim." Neither may you say to a person who is weak of will, "You must want to now." Nor to an unbeliever, "You've simply got to believe." Nor to one who sees no way to God for himself, "You must pray." It is exactly by making such categorical demands that so much of our effort in pastoral care comes to nought. These demands may be quite right in and of themselves, but they may be applied at the wrong moment. Take the nonswimmer again. I must first demonstrate to him the motions of swimming, and do this on dry land. Then I take him out on a life-line. Next I replace the line with a lifejacket. Only after all this do I let him swim freely while I walk along on the shore. Then, finally, and only then, do I let him be altogether on his own. If I skip any one of these steps, my swimming student will find it the harder to learn.

This illustration is fitting in this discourse on pastoral care. The basic evil in our practice is that the demands we make on patients are too great. In too many cases this is so. And with good show of reason the pastor draws the suspicion and even the wrath of the psychotherapist upon himself. Many of our visitors do not understand what we want of them, and many do not have the ability to measure up to our categorical demands. Thus we quite unwittingly drive them into bewilderment with our advice, intensify their guilty condition by our very soul-care, or force them still deeper into their obsession *(Triebhaftigkeit)*. There is such a thing as ecclesio-genic neurosis and its symptoms arise from false, over-demanding soul-care.

Each counseling session should be concluded with a short summary statement, a firm agreement on whether and when to meet again, and a clear directive on what the child-in-care is to do in his particular situation. When the visitor to our office leaves, he must take a clear directive with him to which he may cling until he returns for the next session. Then, at the start of the next session, he will be asked in a loving, tactful manner whether and how he succeeded in making good on the directive.

Counseling is one of many possibilities for finding contact with another. The ability to counsel is both God's grace and God's gift. This fact does not release us from the obligation of learning as much of the art as we can. Love for our neighbor demands it. Only so shall we learn to be helpful to those whom God places at our feet.

CONFESSION

It is not the purpose of this book to inquire into the reasons why Luther's third sacrament has fallen into disuse and is practically hidden away in an appendix to our *Small Catechism*. Here is a fact, though, that is relevant to our present interest. The efforts that have been made in evangelical circles to revive confession were made at about the same time that psychotherapy appeared upon the scene with its revolutionary results. It would be a mistake to want to interpret and establish confession at the hand of psychology.

The place to start is the same as for any phase of church life, namely at the command of the Lord. It is his command that we confess our sins one to another. What is said in John 20:22, 23 has nothing to do with psychoanalysis. This is stated so definitely because ever more spokesmen, in both evangelical and Catholic circles, while not exactly attempting to equate confession and psychoanalytical counseling, are definitely mingling the two. This will be bad for both groups. Exposition of what transpires in psychoanalytical counseling will have to be made later. What is pivotal in confession is clear: The gift of forgiveness through Christ is relayed to the individual sinner.

Thus, confession is neither acceptance of self nor reception of spiritual counsel; it is the obedient reception of what God gives to the believing, trusting child of God. This definition also sets the bounds to counseling in soul-care. Since confession does not involve reception of human counsel but revolves around the gracious act of God, it is not dialogue between two human beings at all. In confession the speaking is between God and the confessant in the presence of a member of the congregation who has been designated to serve in that hour and situation. This kind of transaction calls for a suitable method of procedure. Form without content is empty, that is sure. It is just as sure that every spiritual transaction seeks a form in which it may move.

Form, then, will not be obstructive to the transaction. Confession, moreover, should not be trammeled by religious ceremony. Form may be compared with a tight-fitting shoe; it pains a bit, but it is still useful to him who wears it. This point about the necessity of form must be made because in evangelical company, father confessor and confessant face each other so helplessly. For some 30 years, now, there has been insistence that we must revive confession. Practically, though, almost nothing has happened except in the brother- and sisterhoods of our church. And these have not shied away from giving appropriate form to confession. Withal, the spiritual movements in our church that center in Berneuchen and Alpirsbach have been signally blessed.

The Predicament of the Father Confessor

One may engage in soul-care only if he himself is ready to submit to soul-care. The cardinal point made in this sentence applies particularly to confession. As long as our fathers may not go to confession, we shall not have father confessors. This dictum exposes a neuralgic area in what we call Protestantism. There is an earnest quest for brotherhood, for an understanding that embraces not only the theological opinion of the other but his whole existence. This is good. But it is altogether tied in with the possibilities that go with confessing.

All too plainly a tense atmosphere pervades the evangelical parsonage and can be sensed plainly from various directions. It is there in great part because the bearer of the office in which joyous proclamation is made and forgiveness is announced has no one who proclaims and announces to him. We may dare to assert that presently there are few offices in which, on the whole, there are such inwardly lonely workers as in the office of the evangelical pastor. The dire seriousness of this turns on the fact that this man is usually surrounded by a wife and children.

We regret that our church members are not ready to tell their pastor everything that really oppresses them. But let us ponder what may be a reason for this. May it not be that these members know little or nothing about pastoral confidence in soul-care, and that the evangelical pastor observes it no less than does the Catholic priest? I must say that in my student days and in my early years as a pastor this matter of pastoral confidence was broached only incidentally. This, of course, could be the case in a church that celebrates the Lord's Supper every Sunday and the members take part also in the general (and thus mostly not obligatory) confession, but do not know that the pastor makes his personal confession. Who would be his father confessor? We are inclined to answer this question quickly by pointing to his wife. Doubtless, this course can be taken in many instances.

However, this should be regarded cautiously. Aside from the fact that the pastor's confession will always involve things that touch his theological existence, about which the wife as a lay person cannot be expected to be informed, the assumption must be made in all seriousness that the role of father confessor makes too great demands on her. There are few occupations in which the wife must make so many sacrifices because of her husband's work in point of time, place, and person, as does the occupation of a pastor's wife. The weaknesses of the pastor are evident to his wife. There are also spiritual burdens and needs that arise from the circumstance that pastor and wife have such little time to spend with each other. Burden the wife further with his inmost needs, weaknesses or failures, and you have reason to wonder whether she will not be overtaxed if she is to hear his confession. Usually the wife would be counted on to do this only in a harmonious marriage. But even in such an instance the problem becomes acute. Casuistry does not strike in here. It is simply the wisdom of the church, that has practiced confession for 2,000 years: The seriousness of the matter dictates that he who hears a confession should not stand in close personal relationship to him who comes to confess.

In spite of the subjective interest of the father confessor in the confession that he hears, objectivity must be maintained; and this objectivity dictates that the central concern is not the wisdom and counsel of men but the deed of God in his Word. The question of absolution also becomes more difficult when the two participants in confession stand in relationship to each other, not only spiritually but also physically. It is well that pastor and his wife know from each other that each stands in confessional relationship to a third person. And it has been found good for both to have the same father confessor. But from experience in our evangelical church we know that it is not advisable for them to serve each other as hearers of confession.

A pastor's father confessor should preferably be an older brother pastor, generally speaking, with whom he has no connections in point of service. The pastor should have had acquaintance with him through the years and have some contact with him. However, by reason of the objective character of confession, mentioned above, it is likewise feasible that in a given instance a brother in the ministry with whom inner contact has been made, say, through a book, a sermon, or a conversation, can serve in confession. But when a pastor shies away from confession himself, he will hardly be warranted to hear confession.

The Distress of the Confessant

When we invite the members of our congregations to begin using private confession, we are prone to overlook the fact that this is a most unusual act. All of the psychological principles which would support them in their readiness to come to confession are lacking. We have no custom as to confession, nor do we have a sufficient number of people in our congregations who have had enough experience with private confession to speak of it convincingly. Custom, experience, and usage are the three components that we shall have to build upon in an effort to revive confession. What is self-evident for the faithful Catholic is entirely a *novum* for the evangelical Christian. Whereas the Catholic person knows from experience what a liberating effect confession can have even on physical symptoms, the evangelical person moves on entirely strange ground. The Catholic is led steadily and meaningfully to participate in confession. The evangelical, on the other hand, repeatedly hears the invitation to come to confession, but he is not apprized of how and when this may happen.

Whenever a psychically unstable person submits to psychotherapeutic treatment, two basic conditions have been established. (1) From a trustworthy and reliable source he has heard of a personal experience which demonstrated that the method of treatment recommended to him effects release and healing. (2) He knows that the man to whom he will entrust his own inner self for quite a while has been thoroughly trained in his specialized work. These are purely secular propositions, to be sure, but they are pertinent to our consideration of the distress of the confessant.

The evangelical church member has not yet arrived at the certainties indicated above. And until he does, going to confession will be a leap into the dark for him. In order to help him out of his quandary, we shall have to take these propositions seriously and have the courage to give interpretation of the nature and manner of what transpires in confession. Besides these outward hindrances, our confessant has a number of inner reservations. Is it really necessary that I recite my personal guilt to another? Is general confession of open guilt not sufficient? Is not personal prayer as dialogue of a man with his heavenly Father intensive confession?

The intention of these queries must definitely be affirmed. On principle, general and private confession are the same in the sight of God. But we are human beings. And it may be questioned whether we are willing to go all the way in general confession or whether we are not prone to use it as a way around crucial decisions because they are discomfiting to us. From a medical point of view the question would be: Does the patient seek healing or narcosis? Human existence is such that, understandably, general confession can occasionally stall at narcosis and not get to healing. The patient fails to see why the physician cannot effect healing without causing pain. There is, for example, the problem of painless birth. It is no longer a medical problem but an ethical and psychological one. Joy at the birth of a child and awareness of sacrifice for this child certainly are not enhanced by painless delivery.

We shall very emphatically have to underscore that every prayer can be confession. But here a question must be asked. Is it not conceivable that I may get into such real agony and distress of soul that I would like to have a brother or a sister at my side, who can be a visible witness to me in my hour of doubt and despair, assuring me that God has cancelled out my past so that it no longer separates me from him? In the hours in which "the devil prowls around like a roaring lion seeking someone to devour" it is needful to know calmly and unequivocally that there is at least one person in the world who can witness to me of the grace that God has for me.

Finally, the distress of our confessant often rests on the fact that he does not truly recognize his guilt and difficulties. Much of what he thinks of as action by which he has made himself guilty is only deviation due to illness. On the other hand, much of what we would like to slough off as resulting from circumstances and conditions of the times is really guilt. And so long as genuine guilt is not spoken out and is not forgiven, it is deadly. Here is where the still perplexing problem of discerning between guilt and illness becomes visible.

A much more comprehensive training of the spiritual counselor is required if he is really to serve helpfully at this point of need. This is true particularly with reference to sexual perversions. The theologian should never equate sin and guilt as we see it done so frequently in psychotherapeutic writings. Guilt arises in relationship with fellowmen. Sin is a broken relationship between man and God. The one will result from the other or even be the condition of the other. Guilt and sin are, therefore, not to be separated from each other in a cavalier manner. Yet they are by no means the same. Where behavior is culpable, there guidance can be given; where human relationships are disrupted by reason of illness, there medical and psychotherapeutic help can minimize guilt or give release from guilt. Sin, however, can be set aside only when it is abolished through Jesus Christ on the cross after confession and repentance.

That is why sin is always the center of concern in confession. He who comes to confession has a right to clarification. How is his guilt among human beings clearly marked as transgression of God's commands? How may his guilty deeds be associated with psychical experiences, or hark back to faulty rearing in early childhood, or be connected with inherited inclinations? Spoken confession and announced forgiveness can, of course, give release in cases where blameworthy action has been taken under neurotic conditions. But if the father confessor follows up with directives that cannot be carried out because of psychical or organic illness, and urges them upon his child-in-care, he will be moving close to torture and sadism.

Such action can be the cause of what at another place we have called ecclesiogenic neurosis. Sin and moralistic value judgments basically have nothing to do with each other. They can, however, become connected when, in our moralistic dealings, we come into conflict with the commands of God. It is extremely hard to determine the boundaries. There is but one thing to do: Both father confessor and confessant will have to listen to the Word of God and learn to understand. Withal, moralistic judgments on human conduct must be taken, basically, to have nothing to do with what the Bible calls sin in the Old and New Testaments.[2]

Method in Private Confession

When we speak of method in private confession, we do not mean that there is a set form of procedure which may in no case be varied. Through the ages the church has wisely provided a form for private confession. This form has led to something more binding than does the general counseling situation, and by this form the way has been made easier for a person to make good his intention of confession. The liturgical features of private confession have no more kinship to legalistic and esthetic concepts than any other form of liturgy. It is merely an aid in soul-care. But after making a clear distinction between pastoral counseling and private confession, it follows that we must describe the design of the latter. What follows is in the main a description of the practice that Wilhelm Stählin and his friends have followed for more than two decades.

The service rendered in confession is a priestly service rendered at the command of Christ. This fact is given outward expression in that the minister is robed and the service is held in the church, and there most effectively in the sacristy. This place will naturally have to be arranged for this function. In the evangelical church the sacristy has been thought of through the years as serving this purpose. When used as a confessional room it should not be a storage place for all sorts of bric-a-brac. The right atmosphere for confession cannot pervade the room if a manger stands there after a Christmas program, cleaning tools hang on the wall, and an assortment of books and papers lie in a corner. A standard piece of furniture should be a table equipped to function as an altar and on which lighted candles are placed. Before the altar is a seat, and to the right or to the left and rearward some six or seven feet another seat.

When the confessant enters the sacristy, he is received by the pastor with a ready greeting. It seems indicated that our time-worn and rather meaningless phrases of greeting be displaced by the biblical: "Peace be with you." Together father confessor and child-in-care step to the altar and pray Psalm 51:1-12. Then he who has come to make confession takes his place on the chair before the altar, steadily facing the cross. The minister takes the seat to the side and rear. This deployment expresses that confession is made to God and that the father confessor intends nothing more than to be witness to what is spoken into the ear of God. The pastor then slowly recites the Ten Commandments. After that he asks the confessant to speak.

All this is done calmly, with no show of feeling in the tone of voice. Ceremoniousness must be strictly avoided. Also false dignity must be shunned. It may hamper the confessant as he speaks. Then the father confessor hears the confessant's account, and he does not interrupt as he listens. When there is halting in the recital, the confessant is assisted with a precise and detailed question. These questions are decisive in conducting private confession. They must be kept within the bounds of pastoral tact and the attainment of necessary clarity. Unless there is clarity, radical cleansing cannot come about.

When the confessant has finished speaking, the pastor summarizes in a few sentences what he sees as the gist of the confession. Now, whether pertinent guidance should be given at this point or whether this should be done in a later counseling session must be decided upon from case to case. After the confession both kneel before the altar and together speak a prayer like one in the evangelical church hymnal or in *Gebeten der Kirche*, specifically composed for confession.[3] Thereafter the pastor stands, while the other remains kneeling, asks the questions on faith in forgiveness, and the answer is given to each question, "Yes, I believe."

Finally, with laying on of hands, the absolution is spoken. Conclusion follows with joint praying of Psalm 103:1-13, closing with the Lord's Prayer. The confessant is then invited to go from the sacristy into the church proper, to spend some quiet time before the altar, and then calmly go home.

Probably the most difficult question in all pastoral practice is the one of withholding absolution. It must be maintained that making a private confession does not have as necessary consequence the giving of absolution. In all cases in which it is withheld, it must not be done in a legalistic fashion; reasons for it can only be that the confessant is not truly repentant and is not ready to go a new way. At this point the father confessor must by all means distinguish between will and psychical ability. The psychic constitution of the confessant may under circumstances be such that for the moment he is unable to strike out on a different course because he lacks the energy to do so. It certainly remains undisputed that only the Holy Spirit leads a person on his way and that he is able to control what we have called psychic lability.

But we must know that there are conditions of psychic illness which make it impossible to hear words about penitence and repentance or change of course. Here again we cannot do without cooperation between physician and pastor. Private confession is allowable only when the confessant is physically and psychically in position to make a humanly valid evaluation of his situation and can be receptive to the word of forgiveness. When the patient is in severe nervous depression, or especially when he is very close to mental illness, he is not at all capable of recognizing or of receiving the gift of forgiveness. So if a church member comes to the pastor for private confession and the pastor notices some strange bearing in that member, he must render his service with utmost discernment. This applies also to some of the forms of expression that occur in confession. Words like "devil," "satan," "sin," "perdition" are words that can push a person who is on the verge of mental illness into outer darkness. A confessant in such condition will take them on an entirely different level than they are intended. Should the father confessor learn that a person who comes to him for confession is under psychiatric treatment or that he has been under treatment in a mental health clinic for some time, the pastor will be well advised to consult the attending physician before confession.

Furthermore, it must be recognized that there is such a thing as a certain kind of craving for punishment. This is observed mostly in younger persons. The intention seems to be that this craving for punishment is somehow satisfied by frequently going to confession. Thus a pastor should calmly but pointedly say to a member who announces himself for confession too often that it is sin in the fullest sense when the word of God's forgiveness is not accepted in faith. It has to be considered that a craving for punishment and neurotic feelings of guilt can be related rather closely to sexual aberrations.

Finally, it may also be pointed out that the confessant often likes to make himself "interesting" to the father confessor. Both the very young and the very old are apt to try this. It is hard to discern when this is the case. If the pastor has good reason to surmise that it is so, he can wisely, if possible, direct the inquirer to another pastor, to one whom the confessant does not know. Frequent use should be made of this practice. It is reasonable that a person who has real longing for confession and lives in daily contact with his pastor, or perhaps serves with him, would much prefer to go to confession to another. The pastor who advises a member of his to do this does not thereby show that he lacks confidence or that he is cowardly; he simply knows that it is good to let his members know of the propriety of going to confession with another pastor.

The Roman Catholic Church has long made a practice of regularly offering the congregation opportunity to make confession to a priest with whom they are not acquainted. Understandably, a person will be reluctant to confess to a pastor to whom he is intimately known and with whom he has daily personal contact. It will be helpful if the pastor to whom the person is sent has similarities in nature and disposition to the first pastor.

Needless to say, the parish pastor will not inquire of the pastor who witnessed the confession about matters brought out in the confession. Next to the sacramental act itself, the inviolability of confession is the crowning piece of the spiritual ministry. Its value cannot be calculated. Church leaders who learn that the seal of the confession has been broken should not shrink from taking severe disciplinary measures. The father confessor who has had his heart filled with outpourings of guilt, sorrow, and sin by his brethren will want to speak of this; and he may speak of this, but only to Jesus Christ. Pastoral confidence can be kept only if the father confessor lays before his Lord and Savior by intercessory prayer what he has heard and experienced during the course of a day. This is the one legitimate place for a pastor to speak. Literally, on this earth there is no other place for him to do this.

RELATIONSHIP
BETWEEN PLAY AND RITUAL

Play is natural to every creature and a necessity in all creaturely living. The urge to play is older than culture and art. In order to understand this we must purge our minds of the notion that play is the opposite of work, as though it were a peripheral phenomenon and not an essential part of our living. The degrading of play to an incidental role in life is a sign of decadence in human development. What it means to play can probably be seen best when observing the earnestness with which a girl plays with her doll or a boy with his horse. Both work earnestly at their play. Only foolish grown-ups will laugh when the child is called to dinner or summoned to "useful work" and he makes the resisting rejoinder, "I have so much to do."

The difference between work in play and what we usually understand by work is in the utter devotion and deep satisfaction with which play is carried on. Figures of speech employed by adults are reminiscent of play that was once enjoyed as work. One will say, "This job was sheer play."

At the same time, though, play cannot do without some organization. Look at the animals. Their play is notably ordered, stage by stage. In the *Homo ludens* attention is called to the way two young dogs begin their play. They stand facing each other in a prescribed position, wagging their tails and wiggling their bodies. Then they set out on their competitive chase and scuffle. Thus we see play asserting itself as a force for order, and it is at this point that it becomes ritual.

We are all acquainted with the ceremonial manner of the most modern form of play, of sport. There rules are made a duty. The bandaging of the boxer's hands, the ceremony of introducing the football players before a game, the centuries-old routine of saluting fencers—these are all practices that have in their background a relationship to ritual. Ritual arises from the insight that there are spiritual experiences that cannot be explicated in words but are made sensible in the fashion of symbols.

We know how much the Greek theater with its strong symbolic content has made its impact on Christian ritual. Basically, the Greek theater meant to present the deeper inner drives in man or the demonic forces of the world, whose existence was felt but could not be clearly explained. The Greek actor's mask was known to mark him as an object under the control of one of those forces, of the very one that the actor obviously represented. Greek drama would never allow an actor to be given recognition for his achievement. He was altogether the tool of another and the spokesman and actor for that other person. Whoever was embodied in the role of the actor spoke through him. The word person (per-sona) denotes this. We are persons, really, only in the degree that our behavior gives the tone of our innermost possession.

To say the same in New Testament language, we may cite Paul's, "It is no longer I who live, but Christ who lives in me." By as much as Christ rings out through us, so that our own nature is but the mask employed by Christ, by so much do we fulfill our mission "that one becomes the savior of another" (Luther).

From *theos* (God) a straight line leads to *theomai* (I behold). In the "divine drama" or ritual the fact mentioned above comes into its own—namely, the element that makes for order.[4] Where ritual is lost, there the essence of play will be ceded to the secular world and be bent to the way of the world. We must therefore ask ourselves whether we of the church have any right to condemn festive events here and there in our society. May we not have had a part in promoting it when we emptied our churches of appropriate ceremony? May we not have failed to satisfy the natural craving for play? We know how deep this craving runs. It is not a matter of chance that words peculiar to services of worship turn up again in the world of sports. The goalkeeper defends his "sanctuary." Commonly the excellent performers are called stars. Always the "sport congregation" cheers the winning team for its victory.

The relationship between play and ritual can be observed from another angle. A person who is not interested in sports will never grasp why 22 men run with a ball for 90 minutes and thousands of people in the grandstand follow the action so intently that they forget everything else. The attraction of sports inheres largely in the fact that they afford an opportunity to satisfy the desire to be along in an action that takes place under specific rules. That there are few players and many spectators is not because the spectators are too lazy to play. The spectators are there to take part in the ritualistic action that goes with the game. They do not know this. Each spectator would probably deny it. Significantly, in lands where men are forced to take part in demonic-ritualistic political rallies, sport is given a different role. In any case, the event appeals to and uncovers a deep-seated and smothered craving of man. The "mass-suggestion" idea does not get at the reason for crowds at sports events. The thing runs deeper.

Now, whether liturgy can be useful in missionary endeavors among unchurched people will never be decided at a conference. The proof comes with the use of it. We are decidedly of the opinion that this very hunger for participation in a ritualistic transaction points to a new direction to be taken in missionary work. The church may pass resolutions condemning the drift toward sports arenas and political halls, and she may proclaim these resolutions on Sundays; but, so long as the church neglects forms of procedure in public worship, these resolutions and proclamations will be made in vain. The thing to do at church is to appeal to the creaturely needs of men.

Finally, a connection between sport and ritual is discernible in the feeling that both have for "sacred areas." The playing field has its precise dimensions; and when the player enters it, he knows himself to be in an "exclusive area." At the moment that he is outside the area he is in another world, as it were, where the rules do not apply. Unless one has experienced it in the play-work of children, he cannot know at what pains the players are to uphold regard for the "exclusive area" of their play. The internationally popular game of "earth-heaven-hell" shows plainly by its rules and bounds what are the hidden relationships between ritual and play. A stone is thrown into the marked-out area. The child must leap in after the stone, keep from stepping on the "mark," and set foot into a definite area. The thing to notice is how the area in which the ungodly forces are taken to hold sway is respected by the children.

Again, a player who has his heart in the game takes the game to be reality in every moment of it. The opponent, who is in a different uniform, is a real opponent, and only the rules set limits to the hostility that comes into play. And for the duration of the game this opposition virtually cancels out all other ties between the contending parties. The player thus lives in another world.

Interestingly enough, we conceive of the situation that way; we call that world a world of illusion. This word does not mean that we delude ourselves into thinking that something is there when it is not. The word illusion here designates a circumstance in which we play ourselves into another world *(in-ludere)*. The player is thoroughly at home in the game. He is really interested in it, in the middle of it; as player he is a nucleus of the event. Let it be noted that this state of affairs does not prevail while the player receives instructions about the game and its rules, nor while he learns about good plays, nor even when he is taught in a general way of the benefits of sport. The player is really interested only when he plays along under the rules of the game.

Here, then, is where a bridge spans the gap between teaching and the ritualistic act. Our position is this: When dogma is prayed we have liturgy. And we mean to say that our concern for correct doctrine must carry over into the liturgy. Illusion in play, after all, is the fulfillment of human longing. The actor in a play knows at the moment of his appearance on stage that his immediate environment is but scenery. But he achieves true art in his acting when illusion and reality overlap for him as he acts.

Play demands self-denial bordering on asceticism. It is amazing how young people, who otherwise are loath to submit to authority, will without protest set limits to their usual behavior when the trainer or coach demands it of them. Anyone who has ever been through it knows what an effort it takes to stick to a prescribed diet, to do without nicotine and alcohol, and to do all this for a few minutes of play. When, on the other hand, we consider how seldom we can motivate people to do without specific things in private life to attain to an objective in church life, we could almost be jealous. The rub is not that demand for self-denial is made. Though it may be that the doing of what is asked is not open to view. To be specific, the athlete learns not only that what he denies himself will make him more effective, but also that thereby he renders a service to his team and the community for which he performs. In passing we should notice the difference between a deliberate maker of fouls in a game and the spoilsport. The former means to bend the rules to his advantage. People say of him that he "uses his head." The spoilsport, to the contrary, ignores the rules of the game and deserves to be ejected.

This yields some principles by which to establish social structures particularly for our youth. The desire for good order is far more prevalent among our young people than we think. The outward disorderliness of their lives, of their thoughts, of their dress is convincing proof to the psychologist of their insecurity. This insecurity is expressed in boisterous conduct and increasing anarchy, and it threatens to crowd out the longing for good order. Groups of young people at play give expression to their longing for order. They demand, for example, that the place of play be precisely marked out as the regulations require. It can happen that boys will refuse to play, just sociably, for no further reason than that the table is a fraction of an inch short of the required dimension and does not have the color that the rulebook calls for.

Our intention in these remarks is simply to point out some relationships that exist between ritual and play. Most of us know how play may push itself into life as an idolatrous religiosity. The newspapers report enough of this. Thousands are reported as enthralled by winter sports, ten thousands spellbound by boxer X. By all this it is shown plainly how quickly pseudo-religious forces occupy the areas that we so thoughtlessly surrender to them.

THE UNCONSCIOUS

The Method of Psychoanalysis

Since psychotherapy operates at various levels, it is difficult to give the essence of analytical therapy in a brief outline. For our present purpose we need only to have an understanding of the main thrust of psychoanalysis. The question of the relationship between pastoral concern and psychotherapy becomes acute when methods are systematically used to arrive at the goal of soul-care, which is release. At this point also the danger arises glibly to equate spiritual counsel and psychotherapy. There is the many-hued concept of "the art of healing souls" under the canopy of which the two services are hitched together like two horses to the same wagon.[5] That is why we must first delineate the essence of psychoanalysis as it was developed from its origin.

In the year 1895 a book appeared under the title of *Studies in Hysteria*. It was authored by two neurologists in Vienna named Breuer and Sigmund Freud. Through a description of the illness of a 21-year-old girl, illustration is made of what is meant by the progressive development of the concept of psychoanalysis.[6] The patient had been put under great strain as she was reared by her father, and she became severely hysterical. The following symptoms were evident: paralysis of the right arm and leg, nervous coughing, loathing of every form of nourishment, inability to drink water in spite of agonizing thirst, loss of ability to speak the mother tongue, and states of confusion in which the patient ejaculated strange and seemingly senseless words.

Breuer then put the patient under mild hypnosis and spoke some of these strange words to her, requesting her to tell what she experienced when she heard them. The sick girl cooperated and told more than 300 recollections that were connected with these seemingly senseless words. They were starts of groans in terror or shrieks of fear that she had either heard from her father or that she had inadvertently emitted at the bedside of her father. Each time she regained consciousness after such a scene she carried on with strong affect. She scolded, she wept over her own incompetence, or she laughed. Even so, after she awakened from the hypnosis, the specific symptom had disappeared.

Thereafter every cause had to be brought into "consciousness" in like manner before abreaction took place. Thereby the gift of the knowledge of technique was made to spiritual counseling and neurology, the benefits of which cannot be prized too highly. Proof was given that experiences which have sunk into the sphere of the unconscious can be brought up into the conscious mind by specific questions. Concurrently, a previously unknown fact was established that release from a symptom of sickness can be effected with this emergence into consciousness.

We want to make this clear with the instance of a symptom of hydrophobia (inexplicable fear of drinking water).[7] The patient under consideration was extremely thirsty, yet she lived on nothing other than fruit. When a drinking cup was put to her lips, she pushed it away with deep loathing. Under hypnosis, then, she told Breuer as follows: In the room of her English girl friend she saw a dog, whom she loathed, drink out of a water glass. In relating this she also blamed the owner of the dog, and she did not spare caustic epithets. As she awakened from the hypnosis she wanted to drink, and she had no hesitancy about drinking a large volume of water out of a glass.

The next step was the discovery that it is possible to remind persons of happenings that took place during hypnosis by a definite technique of questioning (posthypnotic reminiscences). Professor Bernheim of Nancy taught Freud that there is no posthypnotic amnesia (forgetfulness of events that transpired during hypnosis). Freud went on from there and developed a specific technique of questioning sick persons (psychoanalytic exploration). He called this the technique of free association. After this Freud no longer used hypnosis. Instead he let his patients lie awake on a couch. He would ask them questions and have them answer with whatever occurred to them. He did not insist on precise answers. In fact, it was the casual answer that he listened for most eagerly; the answer that seemed utterly senseless or even offensive, or if the patient had some hesitancy about giving it, was noted particularly.

In the course of time it was disclosed that the thoughts expressed by the patient, his recollections, his wishes, and his experiences, could be subsumed almost entirely under one term: sexuality. This fact, though, was not immediately recognizable from the data; but with the aid of the symbolism of the mystery cults and the sexual cults of antiquity the relationship to the sexual was arrived at.

Thus two main points were made by the research of Sigmund Freud: (1) the discovery of the dimension of the unconscious together with the possibility of making the unconscious conscious, and (2) the significance of the sexual in the behavior of the human being.

Out of fairness to modern psychoanalysis we must add that the original Freudian concepts have since been developed in many directions, and that some have been put in question.[8] Sigmund Freud's exclusion of all but sexual urges is not maintained any more except by a school of neo-analysts. It must still be said, though, that the factor of sex in a human being's situation cannot be taken too seriously. The central concern of psychoanalysis in the first place is not to set free but to make conscious; then follows the concern for healing through "liberation." The patient is not told that help is brought to him but that help and release lie in his own self. Stating it theologically, redemption is not brought to a man; instead, he redeems and liberates himself. What happens, then, seems to be quite the opposite of what happens in confession. A "sinful" urge is not overcome, but recognition is made of it. To be sure, some limitations are set to the urge, but it is given enough recognition to work itself out in freedom.

The watchword in analysis is not, "You shall not." The watchword is, "You may if you want to." Formulations of this sort are offensive to the theologian, yes, to Christians generally. And they can hardly be reconciled with the teachings of biblical anthropology. That is why R. S. Lee points out the problem of responsibility within psychoanalysis.[9]

In all fairness to Sigmund Freud it must be granted that he did think of limitations to liberated urges, and he thought of them as being a man's own responsibility. But then the questions must be asked, Who can find the limit of this responsibility, and what authority is there to set the limit?

A final criticism of Sigmund Freud can be made on his ideas of religion. Caught up in the thinking of Feuerbach, he wrote of religion that it is "illusion." To this, again, it must be remarked that illusion is a concept that Freud held in high regard. It held no derogatory content for him as it does in common usage. Moreover, it must be remembered that Freudian psychoanalysis, start and goal, measure and corrective, the whole thing, resides in the person of man himself. In extra-philosophical thought no one has given such spacious and deep thought to man as has Sigmund Freud. Only Christian thinking on the same subject has exceeded his in breadth and depth.

Psychoanalysis and Human Reality

Far be it from us to chime in with prejudicial condemnation of Sigmund Freud's work. We shall leave that to people who are only half-informed on the subject. Truth demands, though, that we ask whether his gigantic work is not like the effort of a drowning man who tries to pull himself out of the morass by his own hair. We will have to grant that psychoanalysis continues to score successes in causing pathological symptoms to subside. Neither somatic medicine nor spiritual aid as currently practiced could do as much. Witnesses to this are the many hysterical persons who have been healed, the depressives for whom life has become livable, the neurotics who have been set free from all sorts of compulsions. These all owe Freud a debt of thanks as the trailblazer in psychoanalysis.

But there are conflicts when it comes to the concepts of sin and guilt. When you lift them from the level of psychological speculation into the light of day-conscious experience, you find that there is something more to human existence than becoming aware of unconscious reactions. At another place we have already stated that sin must not be equated with a moral lapse. Sin is an eruption of disobedience to God. It follows, then, that guilty deviations may indeed be assessed in the context of inner conflicts, but sin cannot be written off so long as the Lawgiver outside the ego is known and recognized. The reality of God as God shows up the fragmentary character of all analytical technique.

The aim of analysis is to enable man to find his way back to his own self. This can be of supreme importance, and in many instances it spells recovery of the capacity to really live. The parallel in confession is to let God take man onto the homeward way. This means that a new situation is brought about, a situation which is the primordial and genuine one of human existence.

In psychoanalysis, of necessity, the technique is the thing; and if it is good, the more reason why it should be adhered to from case to case. In confession there is one individual man. In spite of what he may be, he is a child of God. And his situation must never be taken to be the same as that of another. Before God this man's situation is unique. Psychoanalysis shows how the human being is somehow collectively stuck with his humanity.

In confession the unique and individual situation as between God and this particular person is made concretely visible. From all this it can be seen that psychoanalysis and confession do not face each other as irreconcilable foes. But they move on entirely different tracks. Psychoanalysis is a train that moves in the direction that its conductor, the psychotherapist, wants it to go.

In confession, however, the direction is not determined by the will of the conductor but by the destination, which is known to the conductor, and he, too, is still on the way to it. Thus psychoanalysis can be an unconditional necessity before the word of forgiveness will be listened to in the dimension in which man lives in his primordial humanity. However, psychoanalysis can also move only egocentrically and thus fortify man in his hostile attitude toward

God. The pastor may ask, What do you suppose God thinks of you? The psychoanalyst can ask only, Are you ready to follow through on your decisions, so that you may live with yourself?

The Ego and the Collective

Kierkegaard touched off the anthropological thinking that exists in our day. In this thinking there can be no ignoring the conflict in psychology between Sigmund Freud and C. G. Jung. In Freud's view the human being is chiefly an individual in whom there is a kind of collectivistic trio. In the first place, there is the real ego in him. This gives him his essential worth as a human being. He becomes aware of this self at about the close of his first defiant period of self-assertion. Then there is the superego. It confronts the ego as a moral measure of action; by it actions taken wilfully or by instinct are evaluated. In the third category Freud has the unconscious id, which somehow clashes with the superego.

This system hardly allows that we use the term category for any part of it. The factors in Freud's structure must not be thought of in terms of space, nor in terms of grades either. Also the idea of three separate areas does not fit. We shall have to use figurative language. Begin with three circles. Put them in various positions with reference to each other: concentric, contiguous, isolated.

Now for a practical example from Lee's book. A man is so hungry that eventually he takes to stealing. The superego lets him know that thereby he has violated a moral principle. The real ego promptly has excuses ready and says to the superego something like this: Everybody's doing it. Just once doesn't matter. Circumstances had most to do with it. The real motive power behind the act, however, is the unconscious id, as we have named it above; this resides as a driving force inside ourselves and effects the decisions that we make.

Now, the solution of the problematic in the situation could likely come about like this: The superego, or the moral sense imparted to us, squelches the unconscious id into apparent silence. This, by the way, too often is the way of moralizing soul-care. It effects no liberation, because only an apparent "victory" is scored over al-

legedly evil urges. In actual fact nothing more happens than that
a person's deeply affective expression of his own existence is gagged
and suppressed.

This takes us into categories of the psychical. There it is possible
to suppress an urge for a limited time. Beyond that time the id
seeks another outlet and comes to the surface in some changed
form. It is like water in a stream. If it is caught behind a dam, it
seeks new areas to move to. This, then, would be the set of facts
about which so many speak as the "repressed complex" without
really knowing what it is.

It should really be clear that Freudian theories can have elementary significance for spiritual guidance. Of course, the pastor
must understand their direction and he must know how far Freud
reaches, so that he may say at the right point what is decisive in
a given situation. Freud has suffered so much from misinterpreta-
tion by critics of the Christian point of view that one thing should be
said here in his defense. He did reckon seriously with the concept
of an ethical norm. He did this with the concept of the superego.
Certainly, Freud did not advocate that an urge be left to run its
full course by any means. His whole concern was that what he
recognized as the unconscious id be neither destroyed nor stifled.

A Christian critique of Freudian thought-processes may indeed
be in order, but it must not begin with the question of whether his
diagnosis of the human psyche is correct. Rather, begin with a
radical questioning of the superego as man's measure of the values
that he is to live by. Freud puts accuser and judge, patient and
physician, leader and follower into the selfsame person. He also
sets them on the same level. This he does by an illusion of hu-
manism that is either mistaken about the reality which the Bible
calls sin or does not want to recognize the truth of what the Bible
means by sin.

To be sure, not even this objection can be made if we consider
sin as merely what offends moral valuation. This keeps sin in a
frame of reference of human concepts of ethics and justice. Sin
hangs together with that pseudo-right of man to "know what is
good and evil"; and this makes for a radical destruction of man.

Wherever God is reduced to an object of man's speculation, or wherever God is made explicable from creation after the fashion of natural theology, there Freud is inexorably right. On the contrary, though, man can be seen as a being who stands in partnership with God and who is understood from God's relationship to man. This is so when the God of justice is held to be addressing himself to man, and it is so when God is seen as both judging and befriending man in Jesus Christ. Sigmund Freud forces theology back to its biblical basis. His insights are the last and most meaningful outcome of the humanitarian image of man produced by the Enlightenment.

It would be a mistake to say that psychoanalysis teaches that the human being is only an individual. It is true that the men who gave us the idea of the collective were men who gratefully acknowledged their dependence on Freud but never became true disciples of his. We think particularly of C. G. Jung. The standard concept that we meet with ever and again in Jung is that of the collective unconscious. This certainly also applies to the individual human being. But as it does this, it has the individual carry within himself the whole world of the collective which through thousands of years has put the impress of "man" on every single individual. This is not to say that Freud was unaware of the collective unconscious, but his image of man was much more individualistically oriented than that of C. G. Jung. Freud recognized the archaic inheritance of mankind, but he made an essentially individual application of it.

At another place we have already pointed out that man's awareness of every individual's need to do combat is expressed in fairy and folk tales. C. G. Jung advanced a step ahead of Freud by making a point of man's disengagement from his environment and particularly from his own superego. Thus he makes plain that religion is not an illusion thought up by men, but the very core of man's psychical existence.

But Jung's anthropological diagnosis strikes us as being very complicated. In it he has his psychologized religion by which, then, he arrives at a psychologized Bible. This comes out particularly in Jung's book on Job. Even in earlier books he no longer regards God as the God who brought Israel out of Egypt and showed himself as the God of history. Jung's idea is that when the Bible speaks of the land of Egypt, it uses this as a concept for the whole realm of myths. Mankind presumably was brought out of that realm at some point in its development.

By reason of these ideas theology is threatened much more by Jung than by the psychoanalytical technique of Freud.[10] Again we shall have to emphasize to what extent C. G. Jung is right when he sees man burdened with an inheritance of many thousands of years of mankind's history.[11] His explanation of fairy and folk tales abroad in the world is impressively clear. And the insights which he derives from this into the course of the development of a human being are of pertinence particularly to pastoral care of young people.

Where Freud postulates the superego, there Jung sees the sense of responsibility toward the dignity of being human. This may sound quite biblical. But the root of it is not in the concept of the dignity of man as given by the Scriptures. In the Bible man's dignity inheres in the fact that he is a creature of God. For Jung, man's dignity rests chiefly on the fact that he shares in the collective consciousness of becoming human from the earliest beginnings till now. By this it can be seen clearly how close biblical and C. G. Jung's statements stand to each other. More clearly still, let us hope, it can be seen that this closeness is only apparent. And really, the contrast is sharp between the pictures of man in constant development and the picture of man as a creature by a new act of creation.

In view of the fact that C. G. Jung's psychology clearly has closer and more understandable relationship to religion than does that of Sigmund Freud, it may seem strange that we are so critical of it. Here is an irreproachable scholar who by his life's work made psychology acceptable in the courts of the theologians. This was not his prime intention, nor did he have need for this kind of company. But in his research he gave prominence to the component of religion, better of the numinous, as no other of the fathers of psychology had done. From Jung date the first thoughts of the relationship between psychotherapy and religion. He throws new light on the Bible, particularly on the Old Testament. He gives a dominant role to prayer. And in the thoroughgoing way in which he lets you see the great wisdom of the Bible he excels all theologians before him.

In saying this we count the work of Rudolf Otto as standing outside the area of psychotherapy. But it appears that it is C. G. Jung who has stepped beyond the boundaries that are set for the theologians. Among the possibilities ascribed by him to prayer is the psychological possibility of mystical immersion, and thus also the possibility of self-discovery. The God of history becomes a myth. The Word of God ceases to be a two-edged sword and becomes a key to unlock primordial mysteries. The Trinity becomes a quaternity (Jung: symbolism of the spirit).

It certainly is needful that in our exegetical efforts we know more about the mystical realities in the language of the Bible. There is exegesis that demythologizes the words of Holy Scripture so severely that little more remains than banal "reason" that fits meanings to the currently fashionable world view. Parties to it should be very cautious about rejecting Jung's interpretations as unscriptural. Doubtless Jung has more of the fathers on his side than do these exegetical dissectors of theology. He can help us to a meditative contemplation of Scripture again, a practice that we have lost. From him the spiritual counselor must learn what awe is before the tremendously mysterious. Jung really knows what to make of the saying in the New Testament, "In him we live and move and have our being." Even so, when we busy ourselves with the thought world of C. G. Jung, we run an especially great danger of psychologizing spiritual counsel.

We now have available to us an excellent work in which we are shown what the psychotherapeutic technique of Jung is. The work is by Mrs. Froboese-Thiele. She gives us the narrative of two analyses. Both are significant for the pastor because they concern women patients whose malady was "ecclesiogenic neurosis." In both cases the religious problem was the disturbing factor. The cases are typical and the kind that cannot be "treated" by pastoral counsel as it is usually practiced.

Mrs. Froboese, a student of Jung's, herself a physician and therapist, admits that she did not realize how difficult the case was until she had started the treatment. We are granted a look into psychotherapeutic treatment that was carried on with much love and delicacy. And since at no time were salvation and healing confused, the example serves well to demonstrate what the pastor could profit from in his own work. For present in the case are both dreams and numerous visions, and there are traces of presentiment that are the symptoms of a severe neurosis. The pastor can learn endlessly from this. One thing, for example, is the whole matter of transference: the possibilities for its cause and how to manage it. But wherever theological terms are used in Jung's school, there must be a parting of company.

The patient relates a dream. "I came into a room. There, at a wooden table polished white, sat two female figures. The place for the man of the house was vacant. In the way of a welcoming ceremony, red wine was served in glasses. I took a glass, touched it to that of each of the other two; first to that of the mother sitting opposite me (the sister and I had not yet taken our places), then to that of the sister who stood to my left. I then extended my full glass for a while in the direction of the empty place. There the father had sat—quite some time ago. The sister at my side asked: 'To which of the two are you holding out that glass?' I said, 'To neither of them, but to the big secret.' "

The interpretation of this dream says, among other things, the following. The ceremonial drink at the ceremony of reunion at this *communio* is red wine, as in the Lord's Supper, celebrating union with the God who became flesh. This is the blood of the earth, warmed and matured by the sun and in a natural process of fermentation become *Spiritus*-spirit. *Spiritus* is spirit dissolved in water, spirit become unconscious, mother-spirit in contrast to father-spirit who has his sense-image in the element of the air. The great secret may for one thing mean that the spirit needs the material of the body in order to become 'real,' to become manifest at all.—Whenever God spoke to his people, he needed the mouths of the prophets. All revelations employed the human, that is, the spirit tied to matter, in order to come into existence. Man comes to God through reality, not through ideals that are more or less pale and faded out. (Felicia Froboese, *Träume, eine Quelle religiöser Erfahrung?* Verlag Vandenhoeck und Ruprecht, 1957, pp. 128-129.)

We do not quote this to give the lady physician guidelines in theology nor to use a theological measuring cup. And we do not say this in a pharisaic spirit, as though we meant: "See, just as I always said—all's pure gnosticism." We want only to show that we cannot talk that way if we are guided by the Bible. Nor do we need to talk that way. Our office is not to mix Jungian analysis into our pastoral work. Besides, we must point out here that the patient certainly must have had her doubts about the Christian character of the interpretation of her dream. In actual fact, she gave evidence of this doubt in a subsequent dream. Furthermore, we must say that the lady therapist referred the patient to her pastor again as soon as the patient gave evidence of being ready to pay attention to the pastor. Thus the therapist had a decisive part in helping the pastor get his message to the patient. Only, there remains this: Such mythical interpretation can lead away from the God of the Bible and to altogether different gods.

What is this "reality," and what are these "ideals that are more or less pale and faded out"? We shall venture the statement that the "religionless" psychology of the basically Freudian conceptions can, under circumstances, make it easier for us pastors to guide our parishioners than does the psychologizing of the numinous which is offered us by C. G. Jung. As we learn from Freud and Jung in a very, very modest way, we should discover what is the central thing in *our* office: the forgiveness of sin.

Psychoanalysis and Sin

The sharpest reproach that psychoanalysis aims at the church-man's care of souls turns on the concepts of healing and liberation. We want to state again that there is no genuine healing unless there is actual freedom from symptoms. When pastor and analyst meet, they usually turn to the same old weighty topic. Almost invariably the pastor is blamed for the same thing, namely that he contributes to what has variously come to be called "ecclesiogenic neurosis." What is meant is that urges are stifled quite intentionally, that an awareness of sin is aroused, with the result that repression is brought about. The reproof has it that this causes psychic depression, loss of contact, and loss of capacity to carry on with life. There are physical effects also that are bad. Spastic lameness may show up. And since the analyst will not discern between remorse, guilt, and sin but insist on equating them, it is inevitable that he will make a frontal attack on spiritual counseling as it must be practiced.

Basically spiritual counsel always concerns itself with forgiveness of sin and release from guilt. Around this there can be no detour. The care of souls that does not have this as an objective makes itself guilty of disobedience to Holy Scripture. Even so, it must be said with equal emphasis that frightfully often the claims of psychotherapists touching ecclesiogenic neurosis are valid, though they often are loosely generalized.[12]

In great part the reason for this state of affairs is the pastor's lack of pertinent knowledge. And then there is the fact that a larger percent of people in his care than is thought are neurotic, often even psychotic. And with some frequency you meet up with pastors who do not themselves have command of inner freedom. This may seem to be a harsh judgment. We would not dare to make it if we did not at once point to the mitigating circumstances under which they work. The pastor is really a lonely laborer. He works under a bureaucracy that is hardly set up to give spiritual guidance. Segments of officialdom are of the same setup, and they do not know what the work of the pastor is all about. Small wonder that many pastors are adversely affected.

In psychoanalysis reference is often made to the "realities of being." Most often this means that it is false to set instinctive drives and sinfulness over against each other. In this connection the claim of reality is made for instinctive drives, and sinfulness is labeled as an "illusion" in the old Freudian sense.

To this we would say that theology shares in the guilt of setting up false opposites. We may take ethics as an example. There theology has let itself be pushed into setting *eros* against *agape*, even more than is done by Nygren. This opposition does not have biblical basis. *Eros* and *agape* are conditioned one by the other. If we set them against each other, we open the way on which the psychoanalyst may proceed quite logically. We must sort out.

In the New Testament the concept "love" is rendered by *agape* and by verb forms related to *agape*. The concept *eros*, as we know it, does not occur in the New Testament. This does not mean, however, that the idea itself is not found there. It does mean that

Jesus changed the many-faceted Greek concept of *eros* over into his concept of *agape*. It is a known fact that the three prebiblical concepts *eros, philia,* and *agape* are reduced to two: *philia* and *agape*. And so *philein* variously takes on a double meaning in the New Testament. Thus, under circumstances, *philein* carries with it the meaning of *eran*.[13]

Even though the last word on the subject has not yet been spoken, it may be confidently asserted that the all-inclusive concept of *agape* covers the totality of human inclination. Certainly, though, this must never leave out of consideration the previous totality of God's approach to man. And this consideration must not slight the fact that God made his approach to man to the extent of bodily expression, yes, even to the extent of God's martyr-suffering for man.

The deep significance of the incarnation is sensed whenever the *agape* of God is grasped with such intensity as did the Christians of the first four centuries when they taught it and represented it in works of art—though often rather crassly. The Song of Solomon uses imagery in which the totality of the biblical concept of love is expressed. The same is true of certain of the Psalms. The word "imagery" is scarcely precise enough to convey the full meaning of what C. G. Jung has put into his archetypes.

But now to our point. If we stop setting *eros* and *agape* opposite to each other and give place to the biblical idea of the totality of man, a significant thing follows: the placing of anti-moral drives and sinfulness in opposition to each other also falls away. Both concepts belong to the reality of the human being, to put it analytically. Both concepts contribute to the dignity of man, to put it theologically. We shall therefore have to say to the theologian that anti-moral drives in man are part of his very own human existence (of his aseity). And to the analyst we shall have to say that he cannot have a full understanding of the human being unless he reckons also with man's predisposition to sin. And sin, we repeat, comes with disobedience to God. Anti-moral striving is an expression of our human existence which in some mysterious way has come out of this rupture with God.

It should be fairly clear by now that the process of healing is put in jeopardy if the human being is treated as though he practically had no bent toward sin. According to the "dogma" of analysis that is heard so often these days, environment and circumstances account for man's actions in almost all instances. This dogma does not set a man free. Basically, it degrades man to an animal equipped with brain matter. We hold that the distinguishing mark of man is his ability to plan and to act in responsibility to himself. Indeed, this responsibility can be limited by psychical and physical factors, it can be lessened for a time, or, as in the instance of an imbecile, it can be so minute as to be hardly recognizable. And therapeutically speaking, it will often be necessary to awaken from a kind of dormant state the sense of responsibility for one's own actions.

It is possible to treat man therapeutically as though his misdeeds were principally nothing other than natural and excusable reactions to the world around him or to events touching his person. Treat man this way, and you rob him of the dignity which God has given him. Here again the pastor must see the difference. It is his high duty to see the difference between the way that he *must* speak to man and the way that the therapist may speak to him. You expect no more of the therapist (much as this is) than that he restore to the patient his ability to make social contact and to recruit accompanying physical symptoms.

Of the pastor, however, you demand that he show from the Word of God what God requires of his creatures and what is good and evil. At this point a widely yawning gap appears between analytical therapy and the Christian care of souls. The pastor needs to have this fact drilled into his mind most earnestly. The will of God that he must disclose is in contrast to common morality and can be arrived at only by way of Luther's biblical anthropology. On the side of sin, Luther saw the human being as *peccator*. From the side of God's love at the cross, Luther saw man as *simul justus*. Verily, this means to steer a course between Scylla and Charybdis, a course between the frightful danger of exchanging Law and Gospel for moral, bourgeois sociability. Where this exchange is made, recognition is not given to the dignity of man; for to the dignity of man belongs also his sinfulness. Sin is a basic phenomenon of human existence.

But we must be careful not to generalize. Voices are being

raised in psychotherapy that assure us of readiness to be in earnest about the whole group of questions touching the problems of responsibility, sin, guilt, and illness. Let us listen to a few of these voices.

"Guilt and sin are at the bottom of the neurotic person's trouble. In the case of the severely neurotic the guilt may be one of two kinds. Either it is guilt that stems from what is personal or existential (then generally it is concealed), or it may be 'sin' on the basis of wrong ethical decisions made at an earlier stage in life that had grievous consequences. Thus also the neurotic person is not simply to be declared free of guilt and sin, nor to be unburdened of his responsibility for his situation. But guilt and responsibility move from the aspect-level of the moral and the consciously-personal to the aspect of metaphysical depth: The neurotic person must not be expected to possess capacity for self-help. He needs to be approached helpfully by a mediator who will be inexorably factual, who will exercise the patience of a genuine helper, and who will lead him to be able and ready to assume responsibility for his existential wrong decisions that originally touched off the development of his neurosis" (Michel, *Rettung und Erneuerung des persoenlichen Lebens,* pp. 112-113).

V. Gebsattel speaks of the depth of evil (*Unheilstiefe*) prevalent in occidental mankind, and of the inability of any psychotherapeutic school to cope with it (*Christentum und Humanismus,* p. 86).

Quite early, and as one of the first who set out as a Christian to work in psychotherapy, Weatherhead has concerned himself with sin and psychotherapeutic technique. He took the 260 cases that Freud described in *The Psychopathology of Everyday Life* and sorted them out with the touchstone of biblical statements on the nature of sin as found in the Sermon on the Mount. The groupings he arrived at follow: 57 cases had lack of uprightness in their background, 39 "unchastity," 122 self-complacency, and 42 dated back to lack of love by their own admission.

In this connection we must keep in mind the concept-world of the Sermon on the Mount and not the concepts of our moral-world as we are wont to connect them with the concepts of the Sermon. The Sermon on the Mount definitely is not a sermon on morals.

It is liberation through redemption. It cannot be understood apart from the cross and the resurrection. From Weatherhead we also have the insight that very many psychic disturbances have sin and selfishness as their root causes. (Both from Weatherhead in *Medicine de la personne,* quoted from French edition, page 237.)

Thus we see that back of this matter of the relationship between psychotherapy and spiritual counsel stands the question of the person's responsibility. Assertions concerning the influence of environment, of experiences in childhood, and of the unconscious can so easily become the trees behind which the Adam of our day wants to hide himself. "If man hides behind the discoveries of psychoanalysis, he only hides his own responsibility. The Christian, on the other hand, finds in it a new reaffirmation of the power of sin and the power of salvation offered freely to all men" (R. Oderbolz, *La Psychanalyse et le péché,* p. 160).

But what can "responsibility" mean in a neurotic? Is it not medical irresponsibility to introduce the concept of it into the treatment of a person who is recognized to be "ill"? Do not these two concepts, "ill" and "responsible," cancel each other out? In a treatise on psychoneurotics Dubois devoted a number of lectures to showing up how unmerciful and dangerous the concept "responsibility" is when applied to the neurotic (Dubois, *Les psychonévroses et leur traitement moral*). We have already warned against assessing by responsibility. This was relative to homosexuality. And right now reformers of penal justice are engaged in putting this view to practical application in many European countries. But what happens to the judicial appraisal of perversions? Must it not be quit then? And will this view still allow that an offender against morals be punished in a penal institution and, when he has served his sentence, be committed to an institution of healing?

P. Tournier has attempted to show a way in this problem. In his book *Technik und Glaube* he reckons with two pertinent theses. The one has it that man is deterministically conditioned in all his actions. This leaves no room for responsibility. The other says that man has complete personal responsibility. Over against these he sets the synthesis: "Total lack of responsibility in the sense of the law" and at the same time "Total personal responsibility."

This formulation will bear some explanation. Tournier gives it this way (pages 179 ff.): "Before God I am just as accountable for the abuse of normal sexual instinct as is the accused for his perverted instinct. It is not sin for man to be ill, but it is sin for man to be disobedient to God whether he be well or ill. The Gospel looks upon intention and purpose and not on outward appearance. In the light of it, healthy persons commit sin just as much as do persons who are ill. Consequently: It is total moral responsibility.

"And now comes the paradox: When a man is accused in court, by society, that is, by *others*, he will defend himself. This is a common reflex. But this posture of fending off others hinders him from turning to himself and thus from coming to a moral experience. Society means to make him conscious of his guilt, but in fact it is a hindrance to him in that very thing. Now, if *the others*, instead of throwing stones at him, will acknowledge that on the threshold of their hearts they are just as guilty as he, then he will reverse and accuse himself, be sorrowful and have that moral experience which according to the Gospel is salutary. So, if it is a matter concerning others, it comes out as their complete lack of responsibility. But if it is a matter concerning ourselves, it comes out as our complete responsibility." Thus far Tournier.

Now to weigh his opinion. We must not begin with abstract logic. We must rather begin with the reality that becomes newly visible every day. This is that actually we are disposed to think and act in the directly opposite sense. We may for now call Tournier's concept that of reciprocal responsibility. And we may grant that it is likely to give proof of itself in the practice of spiritual counsel *and* psychotherapy.

In a book on medical and psychotherapeutic practice you must have examples. In a presentation of the relationship between psychology and spiritual counsel they are dangerous. This is because it is impossible to reproduce the climate in which counseling took place; moreover, the danger is very great that generalizations be made and that the matter be slapped into pastoral "routine." Our giving of an example is strictly for the purpose of showing what pastoral guidance can be given in a specific instance and not to give shape to a pattern of procedure.

1. Mr. X, age 42, engineer, big powerful type, open to churchly influence but without definite churchly ties. No noteworthy events in childhood. Contact relationships with both parents harmonious. No special physical condition. The patient's malady is snowphobia. The slightest contact with snow causes eczemalike changes on the skin's surface. Snow scenes are prominent in his dreams. When time and money allow, he arranges to spend the winter months in southern regions. The fear of expected snowfall occasions anginous conditions and nervous oppression of the heart. Usual dermatological treatment of the skin produces no results. Psychotherapeutic exploration brings out the following: Mr. X carries on an intimate love relationship with a young girl in which both begin to suffer as time goes on. Even so, neither one is ready to give the other up, nor are they in position to break off the relationship. They agree to join each other in sport activities in an effort to become masters of their individual selves without having to give up their psychic closeness to each other. One winter they go to the mountains to ski. While skiing they reach a steep decline where the girl begs permission to step off her skis and to run. Since it is growing dark and the nearby cabin has to be reached, the man compels her to ski down the slope with him. In a fall the ski is rammed through the roof of the girl's mouth, and after a lengthy period of painful suffering the girl dies. In the psychotherapeutic treatment the patient is given to understand, in a very factual but loving manner, that there are clear though unconscious connections between the girl's death and his "illness." It is also made clear to him that, so far as the girl's death is concerned, he is without guilt, for the reason that it was a happening about which he "could do nothing." The patient's eczema disappears as treatment progresses. He ceases to be depressed, begins to seek new contacts. In the night after he has engaged in social dancing again for the first time, without conscious sexual excitement, a light touch of eczema recurs in connection with anginous oppression (agony of the heart like angina pectoris). The psychotherapist is called in again, and he recommends that the patient visit his pastor. After long and careful preparation, the pastor confronts him with his guilt. He does not base the man's awareness of sin on the fact of sexual relationship; instead, he bases it on the fact that the patient had not been "his brother's keeper." After numerous counseling sessions on this point, in which reference is made to private confession, the patient asks for confession. He does this fully aware that it is not to be a means of cure for his symptoms, but that he means to make a new beginning in his relationship with God. On this basis, and not for the sake of healing, the pastor accedes to his desire for confession. For ten years now this man has had no further physical burdens. His anginous condition has subsided to such a degree that he can quite comfortably do his physically strenuous work. Also he lives in a conscious tie-up with a congregation and with

a very understanding pastor. All this is not meant to be an announcement of results achieved. It is simply to indicate a sign of the goodness of God. Specifically, the sign says that God sustains the purpose for which he has instituted the office of the ministry of reconciliation.

2. This is the young mechanic Y, 23 years old, held for questioning after attempted murder of his father. The father was an asocial man in every respect, who caused his family distress. Clarifications were in order. One evening the young man happens in and sees the father mistreat the mother. With a lead pipe he beats the father unconscious. After four weeks the father is admitted to a clinic to be treated for loss of balance and incipient paralysis. There he dies shortly. Investigation of the skull indicates no causal connection between the youth's blow and the father's death. On basis of medical opinion Y is declared not guilty. About ten weeks later Y manifests spells of depression, and these take on manic features. Yet, psychiatric investigation yields no firm fact pointing to mental illness. Psychotherapeutic treatment is recommended and undertaken. The therapist attempts to dissolve depression by abreaction of a hidden hate complex, and temporary improvement of the condition is achieved. Analytical counseling discloses an association of the patient with the Fourth and Fifth Commandments. The therapist then calls the pastor into the case. Pastoral counseling leads to self-accusation vibrating with affect. This, in contrast to the therapist, is accepted by the pastor. To the earnest question whether he be guilty in any way the pastor gives a clear affirmative answer. On this count the pastor and therapist part company, and the therapist has the patient make a choice between consultants. Y quits them both. Spells of depression increase and threaten his continuing on his job. An attempt at suicide is made. During a visit of the pastor in the home of the patient the latter stays in hiding. On the next day, in a letter, he asks the pastor for an appointment to meet with him. In the meeting Y asks the pastor specifically once more about his guilt. Again the question is answered in the affirmative. In connection with this there is discussion of John 17. Though the young man knows nothing of the Bible, a lasting impression is made on him. The continuing course of soul-care leads to confession, but this effects no change in the condition of the man's soul. After a lengthy exchange between pastor and psychotherapist the latter agrees to resume treatment of Y. At the beginning of analytical counseling he finds a new situation. During the analysis the patient recapitulates John 17 and rests his case on the hymn *Mir ist Erbarmung widerfahren* (I have experienced mercy). After this the therapeutic treatment achieves complete success.

These two examples are not given for the sake of technique in spiritual counsel or psychotherapy. They do, however, clarify the following realities:

(a) Sin and forgiveness are at the root of psychic and, under certain conditions, of physical growth toward health. To be healthy before God by no means always indicates the same as to be able to face life *(lebensfähig)*. It is possible to live the new life with God even though the ability to get along in society has not yet become evident. However, to the degree in which forgiveness is accepted, capacity to make social contact is recovered. When God's forgiveness has taken hold of a man, it will eventually affect the totality of his existence.

(b) Cooperation between psychotherapist and pastor is as necessary as the mutual recognition of the realities with which each has to do. Tensions are unavoidable. The Christian therapist must not simply be considered "good" in contrast to another who is regarded as "bad" for the simple reason that he is not a Christian. However, important as cooperation with the pastor is in the background of psychotherapeutic treatment, it is just as important that the pastor have command of requisite and pertinent knowledge as he essays to give guidance to his confessant. G. N. Groeger is right when he concludes a lengthy essay of his on the relationship between psychotherapy and pastoral counsel with this statement, "Psychotherapy helps, but it does not save; psychotherapy frees, but it does not make holy" *(Psychotherapie—Ersatz oder Hilfe für die Seelsorge?* in *Kirche der Zeit*, No. 4, 1957).

ORIGINAL, IMAGE, COPY
(URBILD, BILD, ABBILD)

Theology's Problem of the Image

It is well known that the problem raised by anything that is related to the image in the religious field is the same for the whole area of the numinous. When the Old Testament forbade the making of images, a new religious-psychological event was occasioned. We know particularly from the works of C. G. Jung that for the religious world an image somehow always shares in the original (*Urbild*). The world of the archetypes, moreover, is not limited by race or religion. Imagistic representations of the painful or instinctual are the same in their basic design throughout mankind.

The recognition of this has given a new turn to the quest for the aboriginal religion which has exercised theological thinking for the last two centuries. Does the world of the unconscious make for human occurrences, religious experiences, and for confrontations with the numinous? The answer given by the psychology of religion as well as by contemporary empirical psychology is consistently in the affirmative.

With but few exceptions, Reformation theology has given its answer almost as consistently in the negative through the last 30 years. Reformation theology is indissolubly tied to the witness of the Bible. Its witness can in no wise be dissociated from the Old Testament's prohibition of the image. Alongside this set of facts comes the theology of the Roman and Orthodox Churches. It veers toward giving a character of centrality to the image and holds that the image may rightfully be used as an aid to faith.

The image has become so dominant in secular life that the psychological involvements of it cannot be surveyed at a glance. It has often been pointed out how the effect of the Reformation was made more pervasive by the newly invented art of printing. The corollary for our day centers in the image: Can it be used for its witness value? In what form can it be employed to greatest advantage? It can no longer be denied that the image makes a greater impression on our daily life than does the printed word. The press and business world have long since taken pertinent steps. For understandable reasons the churches of the Reformation have not yet seriously faced up to the question of how to use the image in missionary work. It is true that during the last ten years the image has been discovered and used as an aid in catechetical work. But the psychological inferences which may be drawn from the nature of the image have not been applied to congregational worship, for instance, nor to the evangelistic work of the church.

In the Old Testament we have the prohibition of the image. But there we also have symbolic use of the image. There is the brazen serpent and the rod in the hands of Moses. Both are not only permitted as symbols of the reality of God, but are demanded as such. The only thing that is "taboo" is representation of God himself. This "taboo" carries over to the very use of language. The name of Jahveh must not be spoken. Was this out of fear that the majesty of God would be depreciated? This may be doubted. It is more likely that the prohibition to speak God's name sprang from the understanding that no man has seen the face of God. Thus, imagistic representation of the reality of God is possible only where God is tangible and visible, where God reveals himself as image. In Jesus Christ God gives himself into the visibility and tangibility of human existence.

As the Word becomes flesh, the prohibition of the image is practically overridden, because God makes himself visible. At the beginning of this book we derived the right of method in soul-care from the incarnation; and we likewise derived the propriety of efforts in pastoral psychology. Now we have this same deed of God as a sanction for all making of images, for all creative imitating, and for reproduction in thought of approaches to the original.

Jesus Christ is original and copy in one. A religious image, however, can never be more than a copy.

This assertion applies to representations in art, to be sure, but to more than to art. It applies to ourselves as followers of Jesus Christ. This is the way of it. We do indeed go to the Father by the power of the Father. But there is this difference between Jesus Christ and our life with God. He goes with the Father as original and copy at the same time. This is the same as to say that he embodies the First and the Second Articles in himself. We, on the other hand, must always look to Jesus Christ's way with the Father and have our way copied after his. Thus the goal-image and example for us are derived from the original and from the copy.

Our point of departure, then, is the theological question concerning the image as this must be considered by a theology that is based on the incarnation.

We need first to have a word on the signification of the icon. Chomjakow states it this way, "If you make an icon by which you mean to put yourself in mind of the Lord whom you can neither see nor represent to yourself, you do not make an idol for yourself. But if you represent God to yourself and believe that he is like your representation of him, then you do erect an idol. That is what the Old Testament's prohibition means." Carefully as this has been phrased, we shall see how other orthodox teachers formulate the matter with even greater precision.

We quote as an instance the Metropolitan Seraphim. He speaks of the imagistic representation of the transcendent, invisible Holy One. This is possible. The fact of the Logos becoming man makes it possible. Therefore the seraphim can say, addressing the Lord, "As we erect a copy of your flesh, O Lord, we greet it in reverence, proclaiming the great mystery of your order of salvation. For it was not in the mere semblance of a body that you did appear, O friend of man. It was in the reality of human nature. The icon is a continuation, as it were, of the incarnation of the divine and reveals the invisible, hidden divine, *even as does the body of Christ*" (From Konrad Onasch, *König des Alls*).

We cannot possibly make such a statement our own. But one thing we must learn from it: Confrontation with the mystery of the reality of God by no means occurs primarily in the rational mind but in the layer of imagery that psychology finds in the mind of man. This is the point at which pastoral psychology poses anew the question concerning the use of the image in Christian proclamation.

The Problem of the Image in Liturgy

The fathers of the church were wont to speak of liturgy as the praying of dogma.[14] We may do the same. But what transpires in liturgy engages the human being in his totality. Man has three modes of perception. These are of the spirit, of the soul, and of the body. The spoken word and music, by themselves, can appeal to but one of these three. As it is carried on in the service of worship, liturgy involves the word, music, and gesture. Liturgical action is clearly manifold in character. In principle liturgy and psychology move on different levels. Psychologized liturgics are little short of blasphemy. Liturgy is not limited to Sunday worship. It pervades the entirety of man's stance toward God.

Even so, liturgy sustains a relationship to psychology, to a general feeling of decorum, and to music; this it does, and yet retains the worth that is its own in a radical way. Right now our interest is in the relationship of liturgy to the image. We know that all statements of dogma have a symbolic character. This is the reason why the ancient confessions are called symbols.

The meaning that the word symbol has in present usage does not coincide with the original meaning of the word; yet, when we use it as a name for a creedal statement, we undoubtedly mean to express this one fact: In our existence we can speak of the reality of God only in parabolic language, that is in imagery.

In line with this is the fact that in the Gospels the sermon is in the form of the parable. This form defers to the mental capacity of man. When it comes to things transcendent, he can represent and grasp them only at the hand of imagery. Thus the parable has had its legitimacy bestowed upon it by the Son of God himself. And so, by inference, the parable that is visual, that is the image, has a legitimate place in the church's service of worship.

Action in liturgy that is imaginal comes along with two possibilities: (1) imaginal representation and (2) human gestures. We are familiar with the Roman assertion that veneration of the saints must in no wise be construed as worship of the saints, much less as worship of the figures of the saints. But it is just as clear that the boundaries become blurred in the consciousness of the man of prayer in the Roman Church. In this we not only see a specific of the church, but we also point to the spiritual experience of every person at prayer who meets with the reality of the image.[15] Wherever there is immersion in an image (meditation) there, in the long run, also occurs personification of the image that represents a person. This is a law of psychology that cannot be denied.

Yet, a question must be asked concerning prayer: Are esthetic and rational perspectives applicable to prayer at all? The intent of this question points to the danger that inheres in the image for the structure of evangelical worship. On the other hand, we have the fact that only a very small percent of people can relate to the spiritual without the aid of an image. To do that we must have either a strong visual endowment or keep up continuous spiritual training. Only so can we have an inner, spiritual conception without the aid of an image. And it is this inner conception that is indispensable as a bridge in prayer.

It follows that we may not dogmatically demand the image in liturgy, but we must always regard it as an aid that is employed out of kindly considerations in pastoral work. For this function the image should be given its deserved place in the evangelical church.

Wilhelm Stählin has repeatedly called attention to the bidding in the New Testament, "Behold." With equal frequency he has pointed out that this is not just a rhetorical alerting but is advice to put eye images behind what is rationally grasped. When the man at prayer trains his eye on the crucifix, he does not do this because the carved figure is identical with the Savior to whom he prays; he does it to displace the numerous secular images that would hold his attention. Imagistic impression coincides with composition of thought.

On our visits we often see objects of Christian import even in homes of people whose contact with the church is but slight. We

find representations of Christ dating from the school of the Naza-
renes in the homes of people who apparently no longer have contact with the proclamation of the Gospel. Are these images kept
there out of a certain sentimental piety or are there other considerations?

Sentimental piety certainly makes little impression in our day.
If we make inquiry as to the reason for the image at that place
on the wall, the owner always fails to give it. His hesitation is
genuine. Modern man is no longer aware of the relationship between image and life as this prevails in the unconscious layers of
our psyche. The representation to which people are partial are those
that pertain to the motifs of security and help. We often see the
figure of Jesus with a lamb on his shoulder. Again and again we
see representations of angels in our homes. Among them is the
picture that shows children playing near a mountain ledge—an angel
hovering close by. Here we get a glimpse into the background of
human existence.

Both of these portrayals make an impression on the soul of the
child which carries over into the sphere of adult life. The representations of angels are mostly devoid of esthetic qualities and artistic
feelings. But the frequency with which they are displayed is re-
vealing. They disclose a hidden longing for images of the esteemed
and for powers of preservation and protection. It is precisely the
growing person and the person who knows himself to be at the
mercy of threatening realities in his struggle for survival that is so
strongly inclined toward images of this kind. Since the actuality of
angels cannot be expressed rationally, a person who has had little
spiritual experience and lacks capacity for spiritual "exercise" can
have this actuality brought home to him with a picture.

But here theology must make a demand of the picture. What if
the representation of the angels is nothing more than a picture of
sympathetic girls in nightgowns? Then the reality of the message
that the angels are to represent cannot give comfort but remains a
superficially emotional matter. A big assignment emerges here for
artistic development under the aspect of meditation. But creative
effort will have to be based consciously on the theology of the
Reformation.

Slowly but surely we are beginning to divine how the image is in-fluential in giving form to the soul of the child. We have not yet fully discerned the force of imagery in the religious life of the grown person. Where is the solution to this problem to be sought? Our first question does not concern artistic components. Our fore-most concern is that we develop a theological statement in the problem of pictorial representations of biblical events and that this statement be truly evangelical.

Gestures

Every healthy person can make gestures. The functioning of gestures, however, is comparable to that of the autonomic nervous system, because they are made involuntarily. Even so, they can be made consciously. That is why there are two kinds of gestures: positive and negative. As one is made aware of his gestures, he may, for the very reason of his having become aware of them, execute them in an affected manner.

Since a gesture is an expression of an inner situation, one needs particularly to be wary of the distorted gesture. It is the uncon-sciously made gesture that is truthfully expressive. The distorted gesture is apt to be the opposite of what it ought to be. It is not declarative and it is not constructive, but it is an effort to conceal and to cover up a feeling that someone is not to notice. Gesture then becomes gesticulation—it is false and could evoke jesting. Con-vulsiveness *(Verkrampfung)* most often goes with occupations that tax a man to his inner depths.

This is the reason why there is justification for mistrust of gestures made by men whose work is of spiritual import. Unless the con-gregation can listen to the preacher with a sense of the wholeness of him, his gestures will be of little use to the hearers. Only when spiritual life has been experienced consciously can gestures help to give shape to that which of itself is unspeakable. Gesture gives emphasis to the word, not word to the gesture. Elementary as this principle is, we are often unmindful of it. In constructive discourse body and soul complement each other. What has *not* been experienced to some degree spiritually cannot be expressed in physical gesture.

This much is sure, gestures can have a proper place in liturgical procedure. Posture in speaking the blessing, in making the sign of the cross, the manner in turning, folding or opening the hands—all tend to express more than words can say. Words operate on the rational level and can prepare for what is expressed in gesture. An illustration may help us here. Take the father-child relationship in spiritual life. It can be meaningful only at the hand of the total father-child relationship in our human existence. To be sure, we must reckon with the fact that in the situation of our families the father-child relationship of an erstwhile patriarchal social order has largely been displaced by a mother-child relationship. If we want to make our proclamation meaningful and our pastoral care effective, we must let ourselves be warned not to take too much for granted. Our people may indeed not have the concept of the father-child relationship clearly in mind. Our love active in soul-care makes it our missionary duty boldly to replace timeworn, threadbare imagery with imagery that is relevant to life in our day.

D. T. Niles did this in an instance which we shall cite. He is one of the great evangelists of our day, active chiefly in the lands of India. In an address he spoke of the security and shelter that goes with the father-child relationship. He emphasized this by pointing to that selfsame thing in the animal world. There comes a time, said D. T. Niles, when the eagle will push his young out of the nest. He must do this to keep the young fit for life. With his eagle eye he peers over the edge of the nest and watches to see when the fledgling's strength will flag. Then he plummets down to intercept the young one. Father eagle spreads his wings directly under his child and supports him. Momentarily the deed of the father seemed cruel, but just before the crash the outspread wings were there.

Think of this picture purely in the language of gesture. When D. T. Niles tells this, his hands are eloquent. His open right hand dives down and under the small, closed left. The fingers of the right spread out to catch up his own left hand. When he used this illustration in a sermon in a crowded church in Berlin, the congregation became restive when the translator (Niles does not speak German) tried to interpret it. The people did not need this. They had already been moved to feel a reality as between God and man.

The church fathers knew what power posture exerts in spiritual aid to the individual. Originally the Christian community had three forms of posture in prayer. These are easily traceable in Christian art. For one, the left hand enfolds the balled right fist so that the right lets itself be bedded in the shelter of the left. This means that human activity (right hand) is tied, held by the preserving, protecting powers of eternity. If you wish to sense the force of this posture, hold the left fist in the right hand and grip it feelingly. This can be done effectively since the right hand takes the lead in activity. Now turn it about. Notice how the game does not come off so well. The left hand has less power and command. This ancient posture in prayer or meditation is a spiritual aid in that it shows how our rash, restless activity is commended to the security and guidance of God.

In a second form of posture the fingers are placed between fingers, and the hands are folded. It is of some importance to know that this posture in prayer has had usage essentially only in the church of the West. Its origin is but vaguely known. It is likely that the folded, intertwined hands reflect the statements of truth in the creed of Chalcedon. The creed states that the two natures of Christ are not mingled and yet are not separated. So folded hands express how in the person of Christ God and man are one in the other.

In the third instance the open hands are held together and upward in a posture of adoration. This practice is continued in Catholic churches. It is the posture of prayer that points the whole man upward. The position of the hands is expressive of the goal that man has in all his living. From the root of the thumbs pressed together to the tips of the middle fingers a gesture is composed that expresses human longing. Liturgies of the mass indicate at what points this or that posture in prayer is to be used. This is particularly so in the liturgies of Eastern churches.

As a final instance there is the posture of the uplifted hands, used in saying the mass and in the liturgical services at the altar. This is the original posture. It was the form used by the biblical man in the

Psalms. And tradition has it that Jesus employed this form.[16] We use it only in the posture of speaking the benediction. This shows how closely benediction and prayer stand to each other. But where in our congregations is this known?

Gestures of reverence originally found their way from the altar to fellowship in the home. But the more they disappeared from the liturgies in the church services, the more they were omitted in family devotions. Demeanor and gesture can be vehicles of what the lips can or will not express. Therefore gesture is a gift of love to another. In our Reformed circles we have let ourselves be impoverished of genuine gestures. We have let a means of guidance in soul-care slip out of our hands.

LITURGY
AS SPIRITUAL COUNSELING

Liturgy in Everyday Life

The activity of the church as a whole is threefold. The three activities of which it is made up are *martyria*, the service of witness or proclamation; *leitourgia*, service of prayer; *diakonia*, service of help to others. They are like pillars that support the entire structure. Each one is necessary for the others. If one is raised higher to the detriment of the other two, the structure is lopsided and set for a fall. The strength of the structure is in the pillar, and the strength of the pillar is in the structure. The importance of *martyria* and *diakonia* is generally understood. This is not so of *leitourgia*. It stands between the extremes of archeology or esthetics, on the one hand. On the other hand, it is granted a kind of shadow existence but is not given an opportunity to serve its true purpose. *Leitourgia* is service before God. And biblical teaching has it that there is no service before God that does not include service to fellowman. The twin comandments of Christ guard *leitourgia* against the constant danger of being made a thing by itself. In isolation *leitourgia* is apt to be given a psychological cloak by which the service is to be made more "effective."

In our day the people who work on liturgy in the church often have to take a stand toward an esthetifying liturgism that has pedagogical or psychological reasons for attaching some "ulterior purpose" to liturgy.[17] For instance, when a church resolves that the

134

Apostles' Creed should be spoken in unison so that children may learn and adults be kept from forgetting, and no serious objection is raised to the argument, then this is proof that the main thing has slipped out of mind namely, that *leitourgia* is a service of prayer; a service in the presence of the King. He is present wherever his Word is proclaimed and the Sacraments are administered. Likewise the presence of Christ is promised for a session in pastoral counseling.

Thus it follows that liturgy and pastoral care must have a relationship to each other. Pastoral counsel is ministering the love of God in Christ to the whole man. Therefore it moves from Sacrament to social service, even though the service be to a cobbler's shop in trouble or to a man who needs help in finding a job.

But now and in particular we must raise a question in the frame of the relationship between liturgy and pastoral counsel. The question is this: How can the procedure in a service of prayer be made an aid to the spiritual life of a participant? When it comes to shedding light on arational realities, it seems so self-evident that there is but one way open to us in soul-care, and that is the way of rational explanation. We strive to use timely language. We search for illustrations that will appeal to men in our day. We take pains to compose our sermons so that they will be evangelical in content and set forth the meaning of God's deeds in all times. This endeavor of ours is proper and as necessary as ever. But what is accomplished?

In spite of all the diligent work at the universities, in theological seminaries and at pastoral conferences we must admit that obviously we still do not speak our message tellingly. Our hearers do not become committed persons. There may be some consolation for us in the fact that in the so-called unchurched circles there still is eager inquiry about the Word of God and how it has relevance to our lives. This used to be so on the part of our church people. But now! Just listen to the questions that keep exercising the minds of our pastors at conferences. They are discussed. Then the conference ends, and the questions remain the same.

How does it come that our confirmands love their instruction, eagerly ask questions, are active in youth work for a while; but when they reach their 18th year they depart as though nothing had happened? What prompts an excitable group of people, who have long since been indifferent toward churchgoing, to become wildly enraged because the pastor doesn't let the members of the congregation sing their favorite hymns and even omits Silent Night from the Vespers of Christmas? Is this attitude really more than Protestant cultural sentimentality in which the essentials are disregarded? Why is it that a congregation will accept doctrinal innovations in both sermon and prayer but rise in rebellion when the pastor makes a slight change in the accustomed liturgical order, whether the custom was good or bad? Why is the bridal couple so concerned that the pastor actually place their hands together, put the rings on their fingers, and make the sign of the cross over them?

Now, there are answers that are simple, but basically they say nothing. One may say that all this stems from a quest for the mystical or even for the magical. Furthermore, one may claim that the mystical and the magical must vanish under the light of the Word of God. But one may also say that the age-old battle between opposites is simply being joined on the contemporary scene, the battle between gnosticism and the Gospel, between man's grasping for grace and God's prevenient grace.

Whoever conjures up the magical should know what he is about. He should know that in all ages there has been a quest for black as well as for white magic. He must decide whether he will recognize the reality of both good and evil forces. The Bible never wearies of telling about them. Psychiatry and neurology are beginning to have a presentiment of them. These are facts that have some scientific basis for acceptance. Thus we must decide whether to accept them or let them be "'demythologized" by a theology that tilts academically at a three-dimensional world-view which is not held any longer. This theological view has not yet caught on to the fact that it denies what psychiatry and psychosomatic medicine work with every day.

If, moreover, an attempt is made to put aside the power of the omen by invoking the mystical, then it must at least be granted that reference is made to what the Bible anciently called a mystery.

And we are enjoined to be stewards of the mysteries of God. The inexplicable remains even when the word for it becomes a symbol. The symbol may be intended to make plain what eludes mere words, but it fails to do this.

We call our creedal statements symbols. Thereby we let it be known that we speak of the realities of God with words of ours, and that we do this because God has chosen to address himself to us in words. At the same time, though, we say symbol to let it be known that we speak of realities that cannot be adequately conveyed in human words. *Wenn ich dies Wunder fassen will, so steht mein Geist vor Ehrfurcht still* ("Now in faith I humbly ponder over the amazing wonder"). This stanza does not say, "When I try to grasp God." Its thought is of the mystery of the incarnation. And this from two sides: how the *Christus incarnatus* can be laid hold on with hands, and how the immeasurable love of God brings this about. To all this, the hymnwriter has it, one relates himself only in prayer and adoration.

We may seriously assume that God has created and favored man in his threefold state: body, soul, and spirit. But then we must just as earnestly assume that the whole man will want to receive this mystery of God's love and also in his human totality make an answer to this gift. And so it becomes necessary to recognize that spiritual truth cannot be communicated by mere speaking; for the spoken word, by reason of its rational character, is addressed to only one part of the human being.

Now, there is such a thing as the verbal character of a Sacrament (theologians have no quarrel with this), but there is also such a thing as the sacramental character of a *verbum*. It may not only be said that a word means to penetrate the sphere of the rational, but it must also be said that a word affects soul and body as well. The *logos theou* (Word of God) is not only the spoken Word; it is also the tangible, bodily receivable Word. The promise is that the Word shall remain even when heaven and earth shall pass away. This means that the Word has an effect which reaches beyond the sphere of the rational.

Something similar is demonstrated in the area of the secular. There is the familiar fact of words absorbed somehow, even though they are not rationally comprehended at the moment. Later on, at a juncture of some emotional excitement, they well up into awareness. A child pays little attention to mother's warning. It does not want to take the warning to heart rationally. The warning may be, "Be sure not to walk on the ice." Then it may indeed happen that at the moment of the first step on the ice the child is emotionally stirred—by fear, in this case—and the warning which mother had spoken looms large before the child.

Every pastor is happy to learn that a seemingly incidental word spoken by him privately or publicly in soul-care has a tremendous carry-over of meaning for the hearer. What happens is that the remark finds occasion to thrust itself up from the depths into daylight awareness when there is a physically dangerous situation or spiritual disturbance. At this point a pertinent question may be asked. By how much do rational understanding and arational reception in the layer of the unconscious condition one another?

Practically stated, the question could be: Is it right to have the creed recited in the children's service when it is known that the children do not have the capacity to grasp what is recited? Is it right to adhere to formulations when these are no longer suited to the present generation's ability to comprehend them (e.g., "descended into hell" or "resurrection of the body")? In the way of an answer it should be said in the first place that there evidently is a difference between sermon and liturgy. In the sermon direct teaching is in order. Liturgy touches man in other areas of his being. And since there is no debating the teaching function of the sermon if the church is to live, we can go on to the nature of liturgical action.

We want first to point out that, quite surprisingly, dogmatic statements of a kind hard to understand are "swallowed" with no hesitation if they occur in a familiar situation, as in a Christmas song. The same person who could not grasp through his logical thinking that Jesus was conceived by the Holy Spirit and born of the Virgin Mary, does neither seriously halt nor much hesitate to sing these statements in Christmas songs. Indeed, he may become incensed when he does not find them in the songs.

It will not do to put the whole matter aside by saying that the man does not think when he sings, that it is the spoken word to which he pays critical attention. In all likelihood this same person would not sing a political song, not even an old favorite, if it ran contrary to his political persuasion. The earnest debate that we had about the *Deutschlandlied* demonstrated this in more ways than one.

In order to understand this particular case we must bear in mind how the human being assimilates. For one, he assimilates rationally. But this does not explain our skeptical man who sings the Christmas songs. Man assimilates also, and much more intensely, in the "strata" of his emotional consciousness—as we call this mode of perception for want of a truly accurate term. To draw lines between the areas of which we here speak is difficult because the realities in question are hard to conceptualize and to define. Emotional consciousness, the stratum of imagery, the unconscious, certainly are distinct concepts; but under the pressure of incoming stimuli they constantly overlap and occasionally coincide.

Take the child or the person whose rational functions are not exercised daily. This person is disposed to absorb things in the other strata, which serve like a wide-meshed sieve that lets certain elements pass through. It is true that the man with strong rational capacity is eager to deal rationally with things that come to his attention. At the same time, though, his rational self may be overtaxed. Then the possibility is given for other strata of his mind to join in the absorption process. The likelihood of this is rather great, and it can come about quite unconsciously.

From what has been stated above we want to draw but one summary conclusion. It is wrong to discard formulations and images just because they cannot yet or no longer be assimilated rationally. Why do we set such great store by rational comprehension? Fear is the basic reason. We are afraid that everything may be lost that cannot be rationally grasped. If this were a fact, we would have to erase from our whole liturgical structure whatever we cannot understand today. This is being done to a great extent. But this interest will force us to undertake deletions every 50 years. The curve of our ability to comprehend rationally can be shown to be going down steadily. The question arises whether we shall then be able permanently to maintain what we call the church.

Meditation as Spiritual Exercise

What has just now been stated will seem new and offensive in many quarters if it is repeated within a theological frame. But it may be questioned whether theological limitations are in order. Elsewhere the decisions have long since been made as to the importance of dealing with the human being in his totality. In political propaganda and commercial advertising no trick is missed in appealing to the whole man. Medicine has recently come close to a revolution, though this has barely been noticed; the reason for the revolution is that medical practitioners have realized more and more how necessary it is to treat the whole human being. Gustave v. Bergman, *Neues Denken in der Medizin* (Piper & Co., München, 1947, page 23), has called this new approach "functional biology." And he has referred to the fact that in arriving at an insight about an observed object the observing subject must also be taken into consideration.

In the Orient all that seems so new, dangerous, and incomprehensible to us in this is accepted wisdom inherited from the fathers. There it is not the property of a select few or the monopoly of certain commercial and medical technicians. The advances made by Buddhism and Hinduism on the mission fields occasion concern. We are no longer equipped to cope with the mentality (naturally not with the content) of these forms of religion. The sovereignty of the Word of God is not disputed. The question simply is how this Word becomes so demonstrably salutary that it makes for healing. With this much said we have come to the matter of meditation.

We are already in trouble when we try to explain the word. Customarily we think of it as preparation for the sermon, as plumbing the depth of a Bible text. The basic meaning of meditation is really quite other than exegetical consideration of a text followed by application to life situations. Starting with the sense of *ad medium ire*, we may say that the intent of meditation is to go to the central point, to strike at the middle, to grasp the innermost.

We can probably get at the concept of meditation by taking an example from Zen-Buddhism. In it skill with bow and arrow is used as an instance of meditative absorption: how a human being may become completely one with the desired goal of his life. The matter does not turn on technical achievement or on athletic proficiency. The objective is that the bowman devote himself so completely to his target and become so absorbed in it that he can hit it with his eyes closed. Reports have it that after many hours of practice the master leads his advanced student into a dark room and gives him a demonstration. He shoots two arrows and then asks the student to have a look at the results. The first arrow is stuck in the very center of the target. The second rests on the end of the first, having split it into a rosette. This takes practice, months of it. Shooting must be done steadily and smoothly so that a glass of water standing on the hand that grips the bow will not lose a drop when the arrow is released.

Or the master may lead the student to a ledge on a mountain, have him stand on the edge with two-thirds of his feet extending into space, and ask him to shoot an arrow from that position. A pale and trembling bowman declines.

The significant feature of this exercise is this: The student is to learn to concentrate so intently on the target that it seems to come closer and to grow larger. The idea is that the bowman no more be aware of the target as such, nor that he take sight at it, but that he experience it and thus overcome his distance from it. All distractions are to be blocked out. The bowman is not even to think of his bowmanship. He is simply to devote himself to complete absorption in his task. The Zen-Buddhist believes that when a man has had such experience with the target, he will probe to the center of things also when he is facing up to realities other than bow, arrow, and target.

It should be evident that this shows meditation to be the opposite of what the uninformed say it is: That it is a technique with which a man is enabled to lay hold on the grace of God by the way of reflection. Meditation is the very opposite of reflective consideration. Reflection is always trained on one thing. In meditation, however, the thing ceases to be a thing about which I think. Instead, the thing seizes me as part of itself; and in it, again, I recognize myself and see it as something that I must have in order to be what I may be.

It is also wrong to say that meditation and Yoga are the same.

Yoga has many forms. In it meditation approximates the goal at which all functions of body, soul, and spirit can be controlled. In Raja-Yoga the eighth stage of contemplation is devoted to immersion. The earlier exercises are intended to disclose the possibility of complete absorption. Every effort at a reflecting "presentation" of the essence of Oriental meditation is doomed to failure from the start. The reason for this is in our Occidental thought forms. They are tooled for reflection and therefore glide past the essence of the matter. Hence, one can really not write on meditation—it must be accomplished.[18]

We have an example of how harmony may be achieved between scientific research and the meditative envisioning of new findings in the way that Goethe worked in natural science. This is true as well of his theory of color as of his work on the concept and nature of the plant. He arrives at the "picture" of the primal plant by "seeing" the plant meditatively, constantly forward and backward. More accurately stated, he "sees" the virtual picture of the phenomenon "plant." His visual attention is directed from the sprout to the blossom, from the blossom to the sprout. At a mid-point he then sees the primal plant. Goethe's letters to Herder give hints on meditative work which certainly is scientific but as certainly not rational. Similar visual methods with phenomena are found among people of India by the name of Luiga-Sharira.

In contemporary thought of the West still another approach has been made in showing what is to be understood by meditation. J. H. Schultz has developed autogenic training and made it a main feature of his medical practice. Through it we can get to the very edge of things by our usual forms of thought and life. Only to the edge, however. In autogenic training, in contrast to hypnosis and suggestion, the emphasis is on the patient's own effort. Basically, this is a matter of technique. It culminates in the person's totally experiencing his threefold self. His experience can be of what transpires in his soul-self when he learns to exclude his mental and physical self. Or he manages to use his powers of spirit and soul to eliminate his feeling of physical pain. In autogenic training such facts of life as fear and security, noise and calm, can be experienced if the person succeeds in making them present to himself, to his soul- and spirit-self, even though they are quite unmanageable in a rational way.

For clarification we can take the instance of how J. H. Schultz leads a man on the way to the meadow. "In thought" a patient who suffers from insomnia is conducted out of the city. As he moves along he feels the hard pavement under his feet, then the soft soil of the forest. He senses the rustle of the trees, feels the benign touch of the warm sunshine; and at last he stands on the meadow where he is given leave to relax and rest. There, in a bright clearing in the forest, he delights in the scent of a summer day, and he feels the security and quiet of the place.

For the patient this is not make-believe. In the stratum of imagery designated for him he actually is not in his home on chair or bed but really where his leader in autogenic training has led him. He, as it were, absorbs rest, and by the laws of totality, he thus experiences a change in blood pressure, circulation, and therewith a freer functioning of his organs. The result can be either a deep sleep or an emphatic renewal of effort in the day's work. Busy people who have come to this point in autogenic training can easily recover as much vigor in five minutes as two or three hours of sleep would supply.

Furthermore, by autogenic training, elements of concrete experience can be transposed to the sphere of the mental. It is quite impossible for any of us to describe the scent of a violet. But it is definitely possible, once we have had an experience of "violet," by submersion in this experience, to relive the whole palpable contact with a scented violet. The same is possible with the concepts "warm" and "cold," also with specific objects, such as chalice, candle, or cross, though these are not seen objectively in this place or that but are experienced only in their essence. Here we stand on the threshold of what we really mean by meditation: to experience things in their original sense (*Ursinn*).

At this point a pertinent question should be asked with reference to many parts of the New Testament. May it not be so, that the Gospel of John and the Book of Revelation can be opened up only by meditation? The Lord does not really mean to say, "I am like a light" or "I am like a loaf of bread." What he is really saying is,

"What light and bread are to the world in the primal sense of light and bread, that is what I am." The figurative language of the New Testament can never be exhaustively understood by mere rational reflection. Comparison with light and bread can be meaningful for the man in the dark or for the man craving security only when he has absorbed the essence of light and of bread.

Not one of us can describe the feeling that the swimmer has when he is out in the Mediterranean Sea and feels the warm water buoy him up and fawn on his flesh. In such moments an elementary unity between man and cosmos can be experienced that is formative but cannot be described by anyone. Such an experience can be made vivid to another only when that person has somehow had a similar experience. We may give a thousand lectures on the chemical composition of water and its agricultural uses and still be as far removed from the experience of the swimmer as we would be if we had never seen water. This is the set of facts with which we have to deal in our concern with meditation as an aid in individual soul-care.

Take the person who has been shaken by fear and is afraid to leave the house after dark. It is known to be a useless effort to give him a lecture on the many measures which the police take to insure safety. Nevertheless, we assume that it will do for us, on sound theological basis, in face of the world anxiety of our day, to *talk* about the fact that God the Lord of the world can conquer fear. Naturally, this is right and necessary. But it is downright unmerciful if we let it go at that.

Such action can be likened to that of a swimming instructor who tells his pupil how water supports a body and then shoves the pupil into the water. The pupil goes under. He knows all right that water can carry him, but he has never experienced how it does this.

A comparable instance in pastoral care would be somewhat as follows. I may read Psalm 23 to a person. But I may also go through the valley of the shadow with him. This would require that meditatively I go through some such dark valley with this person and remind him of a former traversing of such a valley. He may have had a related experience on a journey. By helping him call this to mind, and by relating it to the way that he now has to go, the pastor does not need to make further comment on imagery. His charge will get the meaning of the words, "Thou art with me," and "Thy rod and thy staff, they comfort me."

These meditative forms of soul-care are easily seen as applicable to the concepts of father, shepherd, comforter. If one wants to convey to an older person that God comforts "even as a mother comforts," some experience of the comforting hand and voice of a mother must be called to mind. We usually do this as we preach and counsel, but we do it in a passing sentence or a quick illustration to which we directly add other images and thoughts. We do not give our hearers opportunity to seize the image of mother and to associate it with an experience of mother which they have stored in their stratum of imagery. We push them away from the image with new thoughts and images.

It is quite feasible to give the advice that a person say over and over through the day, "I will comfort you even as a mother comforts." This person will then make the rare but by no means new discovery that inwardly he gets possession of this sentence, and that the fullness and depth of divine comfort are so effectively transfused into him that he can thereby become whole and live.

Right here we stand at the bridge that leads from meditation in individual soul-care to meditation as aid in congregational worship. W. Stählin and others have shown that the *Gloria Patri* originally had this wording, "Glory be to the Father *through* the Son *in* the Holy Spirit." This wording illumines the whole rationally incomprehensible problem of the Trinity. We know that in Oriental communities of monks, particularly of the Startzes in Russia, this one sentence has been repeated meditatively for years.

This statement about the triune God, who will be from the beginning to the end of the world, like no other in liturgical usage, sets forth clearly the interrelationship of time and space, of present, past, and future. The Anglican phrase "world without end," by the way, has far greater depth than does the German form for the same. Actually, the whole mystery of God is comprehended in this formula of prayer and adoration. Whoever recites it as a mere theological term, be that in the liturgy or elsewhere, naturally remains in the dark about the mystery it holds.

The same is true of anyone who assumes that all we have here is a usually fitting conclusion to a Psalm used as prayer. The repeated use of this sentence is consistent with its meaning. God is without beginning and without end, the same God at all times. Moreover, it becomes an aid in soul-care in overcoming the doubt that God really is the unchangeable and everlasting Lord over all that is visible and invisible. Of course, all this is based on the assumption that one must have had more than a superficial understanding of meditation and liturgical prayer. This understanding must have been gained in children's services, confirmation classes, sermons, and private ministrations.

Liturgical Music

Finally, a word should be said on how music in the liturgy can promote meditation. When David made music before Saul to drive away the evil spirit, this obviously was done with a purpose of soul-care. The lad David likely did not know what was intended. The man who sent him there probably did know. This aspect of liturgical music should be seen as having merit. It is not music for music's sake. It is to help disclose the mystery of God. Luther ascribed proclamatory properties to *musica sacra*—much to the displeasure of his colleagues. Time and again he experienced in his own life how the devils of doubt and temptation are conquered with music.

It is known that efforts at mitigating mental illnesses with the aid of certain kinds of music are long past the experimental stage. At some time we have all experienced how music fosters fellowship. We can say of discussion that it pits people against each other; but of music, particularly of community singing, we cannot say this. Discussion is always carried on with the spoken word, and it causes division. This is not the case with music. With the spoken word goes the subjectivity of the speaker. An expressly subjective character is lent to inflection, volume, imagery, and to the positioning of words. In the singing of a hymn, however, objective fellowship comes into its own more easily. Speaking tends to put the speaking subject to the fore. In singing, subjectivity yields to objectivity; the singer yields to the thing sung. Moreover, singing keeps the singer from emphasizing words and concepts that seem important to him. In the first place, therefore, liturgical singing is disciplined singing. In the second place, it underscores the important words with the movement of the melody.

The Gregorian chant is and remains the completest form of disciplined singing in worship. Toward the end of this chant half-tone steps are often multiplied and, in contrast to dominant or subdominant three-tones, they do not form a conclusion. Thus they connote that praying is continuous. Our ears are not accustomed to this. Therefore general use of the Gregorian chant in the congregation is not immediately feasible. The fact remains, however, that till now no singing has been so closely wedded to meaning as is the case in the Gregorian chant. It has been the point of departure for all liturgical composition, and from it all deviations in liturgical singing have departed.

There is, then, the matter of disciplined singing which follows the guidance of a melody. How different this can be is demonstrable. Take two forms in which the Salutation is rendered. Compare the old Lutheran liturgy with that of Bortniansky and notice the difference. Bortniansky has the congregation answer "And with thy spirit" like this:

Here it is possible for the individual, in a very subjective way, to put his feeling emphatically into the wish for good that he speaks to his pastor. The Lutheran form goes like this:

The tone-sequence here makes it impossible to give emotional emphasis to what is sung. In place of feeling (in no sense a negative concept) we have quiet humility by which a petition is addressed to the God who is present in Word and Sacrament. The turns in the first tune have kinship to some affection as between man and man. And, really, it can be sung only by a congregation member who actually stands in some personal relationship to his pastor. Only, this is quite beside the point. In the exchange of intercessions between congregation and pastor the pivotal point is not a good or bad relationship between the two; the pivotal point is in the petition of the congregation assembled before God for the preacher who has been provided there by ordinance of the church.

It will thus be necessary to gauge the whole matter of liturgical singing by the principle of ordination into God's order and of subordination to brother and sister. What is meant can be shown by a simple experiment. Ask any congregation to speak in chorus, "Glory be to the Father. . . ." Speakers here and there will be quite different in rhythm and volume, depending on their mind and inner disposition. Genuine liturgical singing does not force to rigid uniformity, but it does make for a consciousness of congregation in which no one wants to be more than his brother.

Training in liturgical singing may seem to be a purely outward exercise. But since it will make an eventual impression on spiritual life, it belongs to spiritual counseling in a deeper sense. In order to avoid a misunderstanding, let the following be added. There is an individualism in the relationship of man to God that is well founded in Scripture. Luther underscores it when in his explanation of the creed he repeats created "me" and preserves "me." The individual I-Thou relationship has its proper place in private prayer life. But the life of prayer in the congregation is subject to other spiritual laws. Here the people of God in their totality are in confrontation with God.

Accordingly, there is no contradiction between the free prayer of a Christian and the liturgical order of congregational worship. Certainly there should not be a preferring of the one to the other. But a spiritual law of life prevails by which the one cannot do without the other for long. Here is the point at which the fellowship movement and the church must make contact with each other.

What holds for singing similarly holds for the speaking of words in liturgical procedure. This should pertain only to the liturgist as lone speaker and not to the jointly speaking congregation. In the long run we shall have to make a choice between two modes of delivery. On the one side is an individual, hardly endurable, fervent reading of Scripture or speaking of prayer. On the other side is the reverent, disciplined speaking in which words are left to speak for themselves and are not emphasized for the "meaning" that is in them. Against the latter it will be said that it is monotonous murmuring which requires close listening to get the meaning of the words.

We know how the liturgical movement of the Roman Church is handicapped by reason of the fact that the Roman priest has widely lost contact with the spoken Word.[19] Moreover, we must bear in mind that the reading or praying liturgist is not an object but a very subjectively characterized being with his peculiarities which are there by God's will. Even so, the fact stands that when Epistle and Gospel lessons are read without special vocal emphasis on words, the possibility is given to have a fresh hearing of Bible passages that are all too familiar.

To this must be added what has been mentioned earlier about unconscious penetration into the stratum of depth in man's self. It is psychologically false to assume that a word becomes more penetrating when it is delivered with stronger pronunciation. The manner in which a child memorizes a poem proves that words are retained more readily when they are not especially emphasized.

Finally there is this to be said. Heedfulness toward the congregation and the inner disposition of the liturgist are particularly decisive. It would be wrong to set up a similar rule of speaking without emphasis in the sermon or in working with a Bible text in group study. At least, though, it should be recognized that humility before the Word of God and reverence in the presence of the Lord should keep us from further copying of archaic cadences in the recitation of Scripture. For our church a relationship to the Word has been preserved. But we lack a relationship to the meaning of form.

Form and content are quantities that condition each other. The language of Canaan does not mean that we use outworn imagery of a bygone age; nor that we focus our new theological understanding purely on the level of rational comprehension. The language of Canaan means that we speak the Word in the service of worship and, out of reverence to God, do not become unctuous.

One question still remains to be asked: Is the form of liturgical singing as we have it in the Gregorian chant and the speech technique derived from it within the competence of the people of our day? This is a crucial question. The reason for this is not that the modern man is subject to spiritual laws that are different from those which prevailed for his forebears through 400 years. The reason is that in the intervening span of time so much has been lost. Many new starts were made and never finished. Much experimenting has been done. Now it is highly questionable whether we can again make connections with the past.

It is at this point that two leading movements of our day part company. These are the movements that center in Alpirsbach and Berneuchen. Both want to establish a new order of things in worship services for the evangelical church. The Alpirsbach movement has taken its cue from the theological orientation of Karl Barth. It strives to make visible, in this case audible, that the God who is worshipped is the altogether other. The resulting form is quite other than that of the Gregorian chant. Our church should be thankful for the stamp of spiritual renewal that is upon the work that dates from Alpirsbach. There is psalmody of a new kind, organ music that has come under the influence of this movement, and oratorios that have commanded attention. Also there is an evangelical prayer book which has derived much thought content from Alpirsbach. Almost everywhere this book has been accorded ready acceptance by student congregations. And it is noteworthy that the producers of this book risked taking the strictly Gregorian quite seriously in the liturgical parts.

Practice has simply shown that the missionary effect on students of particularly the natural science faculties has been considerable; this in the face of gloomy predictions of failure. Nevertheless, it may be questioned whether the success which has been scored so promisefully with student congregations and the genuine spiritual renewal which has been effected in several institutions can a priori be achieved with the people of our congregations. It is also questionable whether the Alpirsbach psalmody is adaptable to liturgical use by the congregation. The music is so difficult that it must be rendered by a choir, really.

Berneuchen struck out in another direction. At its beginning it was a popular missionary movement which arose out of the idealistic enthusiasm of the youth bands in the days after World War I. It was shot through with idealizing and romanticizing features that are no longer tolerable today. The Berneuchen book does indeed bear witness to the courage it took to make a new beginning; but today it is seen, even in Berneuchen, as having served its purpose. The quest today is for psalmody that stands on the Gregorian, yet dares to grope in the frontiers of new liturgical formations. This quest has become the focus of liturgical work. It takes its point of departure from the partially new form of liturgical melodies of the evangelical mass.[20]

Everything is still changing, but we may say that the aim of this development in our day is to guard the objectivity of liturgical procedure, that is, to set the same before the congregation, but remembering all the while that the thing is not accomplished by simply taking over forms of worship that were suited to people of the Middle Ages.

Every pastor knows that unchurched people are more conversant with hymn stanzas than with Bible passages. It frequently happens at family gatherings that a "Bible verse" is asked for, and it turns out to be a verse from the hymnbook. The reason for this is undoubtedly that hymns that were sung in a person's youth became lodged in the corners of his mind and took root there though the occasion for possessing them has long since passed. Every liturgist should understand that many much maligned hymns are not just whitewash. Far and wide they are the only spiritual capital that many have in the hour of death. We have to ask seriously whether it is responsible action to change this circumstance abruptly.

Our good theological intention with its earnestly responsible purpose may lead to lovelessness and spiritual emptiness in spite of our good intentions. The question should not be whether we should return to such hymns and songs, but rather whether the new theological orientation has been so productive of spiritual insights (apart from purely rational comprehension) that we can really put

something new in place of the old. The time may come when the
catechumens of today may withstand temptation by the force of
such hymns. We should be thankful if it came to this. The simple
fact is, though, that the situation as we now have it does not give
us clear proof of such outcome.

Modern Gnosticism?

We have still to ask in what respects liturgical action in the area
of pastoral counsel differs from extra-Christian practice of psychotherapy and from Oriental exercises in meditation. In autogenic
training the human being is central. The same is true in Oriental
meditation. Man is the goal of his meditation. In autogenic training
he is helped to a consciousness of his own self. In the meditation
of the Orient he is enabled to draw nirvana into his momentary
existence. Where there is meditation, the concern is for some parts
of the body or for some functions of the human being. Or, again,
the concern may be to make a person conscious of his hidden
powers.

From the position of the church it is recognized that these
practices conform to certain natural laws. But in the church meditation is different. There Christ is central and not the meditating
person. In Christian meditation a distinction is made between mere
contemplation and genuine meditation.

In contemplation the aim is to get the essence of things and to
throw light on the background against which the imagery used in
the Bible is seen. To give an example, Psalm 1 states, "He is like
a tree planted by streams of water, that yields its fruit in its season,
and its leaf does not wither. In all that he does, he prospers." What
this says is understandable only when "tree" does not remain a
botanical concept but is conceived in its essence.

The tree, by the way, is a symbol that plays an important role
in the history of both culture and religion. The metaphysic of the
Indo-Aryan is made plain by the symbol of the world-tree. The
Edda of Snorri Sturluson has a depiction of the world-ash and places
a spring at its roots. In Schamanism the climbing of a tree represents a conversion in nine steps, man becoming one with divinity.

And finally, the Bible has a parallel between the tree of life and the "accursed wood" of the cross.[21]

Whoever wants to comprehend this must first of all understand the primal sense of tree. He must ponder the fact that the roots which hold the tree erect in storms are invisible. He must absorb the fact that the tree is a home and a place of shelter. He must experience what is similar to a tree in his own self when he is exposed to the storms of life. He can be helped to a realization of this by considering the essence of tree. This realization is in line with the journey into the meadow of which we learned in connection with autogenic training.

But Christian meditation does not come to a halt here. Man is not an image of a tree. He is the image of God. When one has by consideration comprehended and experienced the essence of the subject matter, then he is able to move on to the possibilities of spiritual experience in meditation.

The content of meditation must be nothing other than the Word of God. We would also like to make this clear by an example. We refer first to an earlier consideration of Psalm 23:4. From what was said there we go on to John 17:11. There we read: "And now I am no more in the world, but they are in the world, and I come to thee." This evidently turns on the concept of the two areas of "being in the world" and of "being in the world no more." It is of no consequence for meditation if this is of a piece with a bygone world-picture. The decisive thing is that I am received by the Father in that other world to the extent that I experience being his child.

This is not a matter of my own effort to transfer myself into that other world with the aid of some techniques, for I may already in this world share in the fellowship that goes with being a child of the Father. This comes about as I sink myself into this word, experience it, and trust in the promise of it. Such sharing on the part of a child of this world in the things of the other world is more evident in the Sanctus of Holy Communion. For the communion table is the only legitimate place in this world where I may adore the Father in the company of angels and archangels. Here, in the presence of the Sacrament, the Lord abides at the threshold as the congregation intones the "Holy, Holy" of Isaiah. This, though, is not comprehensible if I merely join the congregation in rational recital of the confession of faith. I must absorb the promise that is given, that is, I must meditate upon it.

There is but one basic question when it comes to warranting the use of meditation in the evangelical church. This is the question concerning meditation and grace. Meditation is preparation of body, soul, and spirit so that the mystery of God may penetrate us. Preparation for this is not only permitted, but it is expressly commanded.

PART III

The Place Where We Proclaim

INCARNATION INVOLVES PLACE

The fact of the incarnation means that when God bound himself to a physical person he also bound himself to a place and a time. The historicity of God is immanent in such a measure that when the lines of the incarnation are not drawn to the given factors of place and time, docetism has restrained the hand. The living presence on this earth is always within limitations of place and within *kairos*. These statements are not a part of the philosophy of religion nor the history of religion but of the Christological understanding which the church has. In Buddhism the historicity of the teaching of Gautama Buddha is not determinative. The large accumulation of legends surrounding the birth of Buddha is the main thing. These legends form a shell enfolding the otherwise unbearable reality of life. The substance of the legends touching Buddha's birth is reported somewhat as follows: On a beautiful day, at the rising of the sun, the earth opens and gives life to the boy Buddha. The spheres make music, animals come to adore, and quickly also comes the first man, who has been led by his karma to the birthplace.

Obvious as the parallels in the history of religions may be, a complete difference is evident when comparison is made of the Buddha legends with the account in Luke 2. The event does not take place at just any place or time, but "when Quirinius was governor of Syria." The event does not occur at an unknown place but on the way from Nazareth to Bethlehem. The wise men are not led by karma but by comets moving in time and space. Textual criticism on Luke 2 changes nothing in our consideration. We need but mark that, quite apart from exegetical correctness, there is in the background a clear indication that neither the crib nor the persons present are central—only Christ as he becomes flesh and simultaneously binds himself to place and time.

Much of the Gospel of John becomes transparent only when the *logos theou* is not only *en sarki* but also *en kairo*. There once was a time when the people on the streets of Capernaum and Jerusalem could say, "Behold, this is the lamb of God." Or, "And he remained with him unto the tenth hour." Everything in the life of Jesus, like the light of lightning, is an anticipation of the glory of God that is to be revealed at his return; but equally it posits that God is visible in space and time. Hundreds of sick persons wait for healing at the Pool of Bethesda. Only once is the power of the Son of God demonstrated as it is to be experienced by the world at his return. To just one man does Jesus reveal what will happen for those who are asleep in Christ at his return. Hundreds hear him preach, but few realize for a short time what will be revealed to the world on that day, namely: Christ, the Lord of the world. For the moment when he breaks the bread the disciples recognize the presence of the risen Lord. In the next moment all is as before.

If there is a continuing and apostolic proclamation of the message of God, if the sacramental presence of God is taken seriously, then this promise of the presence under Word and Sacrament must somehow include the categories of space and time, even as Jesus tied himself to these categories while he was on earth, and as the promise of a new heaven and a new earth in no way eliminates these categories. From these facts we have to go on to raise and answer questions as they pertain to time and place of worship.

THE PLACE OF WORSHIP

In his *Leiturgia I*, Langmaack has explicitly and convincingly given us the architectural and historic features of the place of divine worship. Now it can no longer be said that the significance of the place of worship is but an incidental matter for the history of dogma and church. Moreover, if it is true that the Holy Spirit leads us into all truth, then it is also true that these two subjects cannot be taught in evangelical schools without acknowledging that the work of the Holy Spirit can be discerned in the history of dogma and church. However, we shall not now develop the problem of the place of worship from the aspect of history and liturgy. We shall try to see what pastoral psychology may have to say about the place or worship. From what has been set forth above it should be clear that in this matter our concern is not with the esthetic nor primarily with the liturgical. We are interested in the implications which occur when the doctrine of the incarnation is earnestly instated.

Evidence has it that already in the reign of Hadrian, Christians made a start in devising a style for the place of worship.[1] There came a time when the Hall of Solomon could no longer be used. But Christians were wont to meet at regular places, and the presumption can be made that they met for congregate worship. Thus, already near 130 A.D. there were sacred buildings designed particularly for such worship.

By the third century these buildings had taken a definite form.

Procedure in worship had been developed sufficiently to demand a definite style for the place of worship. San Theodoro in Ravenna probably is the only place of worship of the ancient church that still exists. It dates from 206 A.D. and antedates the Constantinian era.

When, with the recognition of Christianity by Constantine, all restrictions were lifted, including those on the design of buildings, the basic form of the church building had already been established. Thus there was no need to create one. That form is known as the basilica. Its characteristic foundation design is that of the cross. In order to arrive at the meaning of this building's form one must meditate upon it. It is not by chance that the altar stands at the place where on the foundation design of the cross the Redeemer's head was positioned on his cross. Neither was it by chance that churches were oriented early in their history. The sacred place has to be entered on foot. The place invites entry to be made at the foot of the cross. Advancement is made past the intersection of the two beams of the cross to fellowship with Christ at the altar.

We see from this that the ancient church had already thought of the structure of the church building as a requisite aid to meditation and built churches with that purpose in mind. How much more should we be able to do the same when strangers to the Gospel come to our churches: lead them from the narthex to the altar, and as we do this lead them to a knowledge of Christ! Wherever the totality of the human being is held in mind, there must not be a calculated neglect or an oversight of what most totally pertains to him, namely the God-man relationship. For a practical instance this could mean that during the first hour of meeting with his catechumens the pastor should tour the floor of the church with his class. This good practice would be worthless if the pastor himself has never made such a thoughtful pilgrimage from entryway to the altar. And our godparents, our bridal couples, our confirmands—what do they truly know of the intense reality of the event when the pastor leads them to the altar? Indeed, if this procession is nothing more than a pompous, festal march for the gaping public to be astonished at, if neither bridal couple nor catechumens have had their eyes opened to the significance of such a solemn procession, the whole thing can turn out to be nothing more than sentimental liturgism. We would then be well advised to get rid of it forthwith.

Certain as it is that the grace of God can meet us at any moment of life, and certain as it is that meeting with God is not of our effort nor of any psychological-liturgical technique, it is just as certain that we who are to be stewards of the mysteries of God dare not hide these mysteries from the congregation. Consequently, the first demand that should be made of the church building is that this meaning meet the eye of the congregation in all feasible details. A helpful measure to take could be to have all doors to the place closed except the one at the main entrance, which is directly opposite the altar.

The three essential parts of the basilica are nave, choir, and apse. If one has never sensed that tarrying in the nave of the church is truly expressive of the church riding out a storm in the midst of the sea, he will hardly be able to move into the security of the ongoing service before God. Anyone who has not yet felt what the walls and the door of the church say about the relationship of the Christian to the world, will inevitably fall victim to a ghetto existence or sheer secularization. To sit in the nave of the church means to experience anew the stilling of the storm in all its phases as each service of worship runs its course. It will then also be discerned that the shelter of the sacred place has no part with the neat complacency of the bureaucracy of occasional church-goers. But then it also becomes clear that the security of the nave of the church conquers a certain anxiety. This is the anxiety which prompts, in a kind of spiritual prostitution, to yielding to the world under all circumstances. For this, so quickly, the misused saying about the church's service to the public is used as a cloak.

From the nave of the church the way leads to the choir. Our choirs will be used as musical "inserts" until the vicarious character of the choirs is made plain and demonstrable to the congregation. In the first place, the choir has been that portion of the congregation assigned to render a definite part of the service of worship in behalf of the congregation. Whoever believes that vicarious action was taken only on Golgotha and in this world only for Christians is mistaken about the mystery of the continuing presence of the body of Christ in the world. Two things are quite self-evident here. The one is that the church acts vicariously before God for the world and does what the world either cannot or will not do. The other is that within the structure of a service of worship the choir acts vicariously in adoration of the Lord who is present in Word and Sacrament. This vicarious function, however, must become as discernible as God's vicarious work on Golgotha has become discernible. For this reason it is necessary to recover the meaning which the choir area has by reason of its position and relationship.

When the reforming fathers removed the screen which excluded the congregation from the altar area, they acted wisely. With the rending of the veil in the Temple the screen also fell away. Thus we cannot possibly concur with the Roman Church when it places the altar area, architecturally and liturgically, on a level other than that of the nave and the choir area. At the same time we shall have to learn to understand the significance of the place of the altar. In John 1 the reality of the incarnation as it touches all realms of the visible and invisible world is expounded. In Christ there is a "Behold here!" So there is a place where the congregation may see as clearly as a flash of lightning a "Behold here!" This is where the Sacrament is celebrated. Evangelical understanding has it that the altar is not a place of magical transubstantiation and not the holiest place in comparison with other parts of the church, as though they were less sacred. The altar is a table and nothing more. At the same time, however, the altar is the very place from which Word and Sacrament go forth, which makes it the place of the real presence. Hence it is no less than the place at which the celebrating congregation perceives the reality of the presence of Christ—though never *a se*, never without Word and Sacrament

The problem of the image in the service of worship arises anew when a place of worship is being planned. In this we seem to be ready to rediscover some things that have been lost. It may therefore be indicated that some definite outlines be drawn, though very gropingly and ever so cautiously. In any case, there can be no invoking the Old Testament prohibition of graven images. The incarnation itself stands for the imageability of God, and God himself executed that image. Right here a further question arises. When it comes to the matter of the picture, to what extent will Christocentric theology of our day be consistent in accepting the incarnation? Our main concern is not whether a work of art be "conceptual" or "abstract." A valid criterion serves well here: Count that good "which treats of Christ." Certainly, the Christ of Christmas, Good Friday, and Easter. The church knows no other Christ. Whatever more can be said we shall presume to hint at in questions only.

May a work of art be placed in the church which is so composed that its meaning can be arrived at only by sustained meditation? Or must it be directly comprehensible and receivable in the imagination so that it prepares the soil for the seed of the preached Word?

Is it allowable that the picturesque design of the church window use light effects of the sun to the greater glory of God in recognition of the fact that the sun also declares "the work of his hands"?

Or is it forbidden to employ creation's glory as exhibited in the cosmos in support of the preached Word?

Is it possible that at long last works of art may recommend themselves which require meditation to be comprehended and intelligence to be understood?

Here are the works of boundless beauty which new church art is offering. What about them and the well-nigh radical rejection of them by the congregation? What about the rift between artist and congregation? Is it not the greater because, through the years, congregations have not appreciated the beautiful services of worship for lack of interpretation? May it not be that the gap between artistic creativity and our congregations' appreciation is so great because the grace of God has led but a small company of men up the Mount of Transfiguration while, by and large, our congregations —equally by the counsel of God—did not get up there? But then, who must yield to whom?

Our new theological considerations are a definite advantage. We must be grateful as we receive them from the hand of God. But, in spite of them, we have suffered "the loss of the mean (middle)." This is most evident when we face up to the prevalent lack of understanding of what it takes to put together a sacred place of worship.[2]

MEETING PLACES
FOR THE CONGREGATION

Ruined churches are still to be found in Germany. This fact should be favorable to realizing the proposals which have been made. Certainly it was not apart from God's doing that this situation came about. Ought we not, as builders of new church structures, think of getting beyond "by the Word alone" and live "from out of the Word"? Does not the experience of our everyday churchly living make us wonder whether our deliberations are not of some piece with magical speculations, or whether we are not operating with a modern form of gnosticism in biblical guise? To be sure, the frequency with which such questions are being asked proves nothing as to their correctness. But more than ever we are today duty bound to be open to questions. Are we of the church not in danger of using psychological insights to bypass tasks that stand before us?

Two facts stand firm: The problem of the place of worship will not be solved by the Word; yet this problem must not be viewed apart from the Word. Also, we must be mindful that we never have this Word in the abstract. Always it is the Word become flesh, that has taken on form. The disastrous separation of Word and Sacrament has in our day become an occasion for a veritable confrontation in theology. This separation misses the fact that we always have to do with the Word become flesh.

The results of this show up in places of worship, not only in the design of the domes built in the early Middle Ages but also in the

congregation centers of our day. Anyone who builds centers for congregations from the standpoint of utility and has in view nothing
more than the number of people that he may eventually accom-
modate, or who provides areas for confirmands and youth with no
further purpose than the "functional" in pedagogical procedure
should not be surprised when the proclamation of the Word become
flesh turns up as moral and ethical religion that is quite inter-
changeable with secular varieties of religion. Substance creates
forms for itself. One needs only to have seen the Congress Hall of
the Third Reich, or the house of cultural workers in East Berlin,
or the memorial buildings for the leaders in dialectical materialism;
he will ever after want to have very good reasons before he departs
from basic laws of sacred design. A misunderstood purpose of the
structure will not be sufficient reason for departure from sacred
design. This applies not only to the church for worship but to the
whole church plant.

The congregation center has an advantage over the church building of traditional style in that it can exhibit the many offices pointed
to in 1 Corinthians 12. The very spatial structure can excel its ante-
cedents in expressing the priestly action of the church in the world.
When new churches are built, the opportunity should be seized
upon to achieve not only good structure but especially sacred
design.

The laying out of a ground plan is the business of the architect.
But it is the concern of pastoral psychology to integrate the many
offices of the congregation with its chief office and to make visible
what is auxiliary to that chief office; in short, it is to exhibit a new
understanding of what is "church." Essentially, the outcome appears to be that the place of worship be kept at the center (mid-
most) and that there be exits from it to areas for instruction, for
youth work, or for other endeavors of the congregation. Thus, by
force of the structure, the congregation moves from its central life of
worship to its missionary, apostolic errands as a genuine, universal
priesthood. Or, the other way around, the way leads from preparation for work in the congregation to its center, that is, to the place
of worship which is the central part of all.

It may be fitting to mention that this arrangement reproduces the design of a dwelling place in apostolic times. The basic plans of private dwellings, which served as places of meeting for the early Christians, display the same principle. This has been shown by Langmaack. When it comes to the place of worship, there must be no eliminating of the features to which reference has been made earlier. Nave, choir area, altar space, must not only be retained, but they must be distinctively marked off for visitors to see. This may be done by meaningful placing of pews, by choice of color on the walls, or by actual location of choir area forward and including a small organ.

There is also a growing understanding in the congregation that you do not use every place for whatever purpose. When the problem of shortage of space has to be solved for an occasion, the consideration must be that this be done in such a way as to create an atmosphere expressive of the Word become flesh—this time in the sense of the Third Article. The time should be long past when the whitewashed area with its cross on the one side and the Luther picture on the other represents the alpha and omega of evangelical arrangement of the place. A church cannot become a home when the place in which people are called together is more like the waiting room of a business office than like the vessel that holds the message of the love of God to man.

Let us now turn our attention to the area for youth. The first things to determine are whether this is to be for groups of children or of youth and whether it is to be for youth of both sexes. It should also be determined whether it is to be an area in which regular instruction hours are to be held or whether it is to be in the order of a home for youth to which young people may come at any time, where they may spend free time to their hearts' content. When it comes to rooms for the kindergarten children, the requirements are understood and accepted everywhere. But our church councils and elders have hardly thought of what is required for youth work in the way of arrangements. Facilities for lighting and heating can be taken for granted. The crucial thing is the choice of pictures. What has been stated earlier in the way of theory on the worth of goal-images has practical pertinence here. Pictorial art has given us a number of works that may be deemed to have timeless validity.

Duerer's *Knight, Death, and the Devil* is one of them. Others are the figure of *Uta* at Naumburg and *The Rider* of Bamberg.

Of modern art, Marc's paintings of the gazelle and the tiger may be counted as appropriate. Given introductory interpretation, the works of the Blue Rider group are acceptable. These paintings do not belong to the class that is usually spoken of as "churchly art." At this point something should be said in addition to the uncounted statements already made on what constitutes churchly art, if there is such a distinct thing. Going out from the problem of the goal-image, it must be held that a picture always touches a reality which has been received in the inmost being of man and is given shape there by what of itself is abstract. Duerer's *Knight, Death, and the Devil* can then become a guiding figure for the youth in the problems of his developing self. The maidenly and at the same time womanly coyness of a *Uta* can be a goal-image for the girl. The pictures by Marc which have been cited can serve to explain assertions about Creator and creature. There is, for example, in the picture of the tiger an overlapping of planes of existence made visible in the background.

Nothing impresses more tellingly than do pictures. The selection of them for church rooms is a real duty of a pastor in his work. And if he will, as need requires, consult with a mature member of his congregation, or have that member make selection of a suitable picture, a practical demonstration will be made of what is meant by the universal priesthood. It will not require a person who is versed in the history of art, nor an architect who resides in the congregation, but a person for whom every picture of a creature is a parabolic image of that creature in its dependence upon the Creator.

The answer to the question concerning Bible verses points in the same direction. It makes good sense to keep the same text in the place where the congregation worships, be it placed over the altar or elsewhere. In the room for youth, on the other hand, the effectiveness of a repeated reading of a text levels off and then fails of its objective. This is because it may so easily be taken as belonging to what seems to be a "daubing on of piety." Bible verses for the week or for the month are good. A selection of good sayings like the well-known "golden words" continue to be the most useful.

As for the other appointments in the room for youth, a middle course should be steered between what the young experience in life in point of color and form and what is not in too great contrast to their homes and place of worship. To all appearances, with all our efforts, we have not yet found the middle course in arranging proper settings for our youth. The course should be between the luxurious and a poverty that is simply unbearable in an atmosphere that is deadening. Curtains, tapestry, colors, and carpeting hinge on the uses to which the room is to be put.

These principles apply similarly to rooms that are used for other work of the congregation. It is deplorable that it must still be emphasized that ashtrays are not the properties of a satanic culture. One should notice how shyly men light their cigarettes on a night at church after a nerve-straining workday of 10 or 12 hours and understand that they simply cannot follow the proceedings further unless they do. One should understand that a general prohibition of smoking at congregational group meetings has no biblical basis but is much rather based on unbiblical lack of love. It may be that much can be said against "socials" that are held after almost every service of worship in England and America. Yet it should not be impossible, particularly in the big city congregations, to invite the congregation to gather in a suitable room for a sociable get-together. If one has experienced in what ways the results of the sermon can be noticed as he becomes acquainted with hearers in a natural, altogether personal way over a cup of tea and a cigarette, he will have serious second thoughts before he turns down such efforts as tending toward the secular. Brotherhood wants to be expressed in a corporeal form.

It is one of the grave failings of Protestantism that it halts at half-measures when it comes to the corporeal realization of what has been thought out theologically and quite formally. Small congregations should by all means ascertain whether they may not have a place in their churches where people can be together after worship or Bible study in an informal way without the trammel of a "pious program." In light of this it is a real question whether a kitchen may not be a necessary adjunct to every congregation's plant, yes, to each larger hall there.

It is necessary that we tarry a while on the appointments that should go into the room for the catechumens. Classroom atmosphere is ruinous in the room for the confirmation class. A large share of the disciplinary problem that a pastor has with his class goes back psychologically to the fact that the room invites to doing in the confirmation hour what is done in the classroom at school. And since rowdy behavior is less risky here than at school, there can be small wonder that much use is made of the opportunity to stir up mischief. If the pastor or his helper is seen in the role of teacher, it is the more difficult from the start to place the accent on pastoral care. The modern classroom has quite wisely had its rigid seating order broken up, and it has become a purposeful livingroom. To the extent that confirmation instruction differs from instruction at school in room arrangement, pedagogical technique, and formal structure, to that extent the possibility increases to make it what it is intended to be. Thus, if at all possible, there should be no neatly arranged rows of school desks where children take their places in alphabetical order, but chairs and tables at which to sit, and the pastor in the midst of them. And by no means should there be raising of hands or rising—answers are to be given from the sitting position. And in small groups free conversation can occasionally be allowed, even encouraged. All this does not make for disciplinary burdens but eases the pastor's work greatly.

It is obvious that a room must be appropriately appointed for such use. Colorful curtains, but no lectern and no stick to point with. The weekly verse to be learned may be put up on the wall and together with various pictures that are related to the subject to be studied. Practically, it will rarely be possible to have confirmation instruction and youth work in separate rooms. Where this is possible, it should definitely be done.

In wide areas of public life it is recognized that space and room arrangements are helpful in work of every kind. The calming effect of color has long been known in medical practice. We put dark blue or green tile on the walls of operating rooms; we give the sickrooms a light color and avoid garish white; and we know of the quieting effect of pictures. It is high time that these principles be employed in planning work areas in churches. This is not a matter with which

people of specialized interest play around; it is a matter of earnestness in our obligations as pastor. We want to give people every
inducement to come to us. Unless a man who preaches the Savior
also does what he can to make wholesome the place where people
are gathered for this preaching, he will hardly carry the conviction
that he is serving as a pastor for the sake of the Savior whom he
preaches. What is involved here is not something that you can take
or leave; nor is it debatable. The thing turns on sober, clear insights
granted us by him who has given us "and still preserves to us our
reason and all our senses."

PLACES FOR COUNSELING
AND CONFESSION

At the outset it should be said that the principles for sacred design apply as well in the small as in the large counseling room. But now we come to a factor that cannot be put into words so easily and for which we shall use the concept of "atmosphere" conducive to pastoral counsel. What transpires at the parsonage often puts one in mind of what goes on at a well-run office. The reason for this is neither evil intent nor lack of love. Rather, the reason for it is either a lack of knowledge of certain psychological laws or a strange striving to function like an efficient office.

The beginning of this is often made when the visitor rings the doorbell and is overwhelmed by the pastor's wife or the parish worker who says, "What business may you have with the pastor?" Or even, "Whom may I announce?" It is quite clear, we should hope, that such a manner of reception can crush the purpose which motivated the visitor to seek out the pastor.

Let us repeat that in our time it is not self-evident that a clergyman be visited for reasons other than to ask for some ministerial act or to make such need known as is reported to a social service agency. In every case a person may have had an inner struggle for weeks before he resolved to see his pastor in a matter touching the care of his soul. It is therefore mandatory that clergymen and parish workers courteously accept every opportunity that offers itself for pastoral counseling.

Does this indicate that office hours for such engagements be posted at the entrance to the parsonage? It is told of the sainted bishop Ihmels that he once stood before such a posted schedule and pondered a while. Then he reached into his pocket for his New Testament. The pastor stood by his side and repeatedly asked what he might be looking for. Each time he received the answer, "I don't find it here, I don't find it." Finally the bishop laid his hand on the pastor's shoulder and spoke these classic words, "I cannot find the passage in which the Lord Jesus posted his hour for counseling."

Now, it does not follow strictly from the gist of this anecdote that a pastor must be available for counseling early and late. This is sometimes asserted in theological lectures. That is neither right nor suitable. In fact, it is impossible. What seems more convincing to me is the advice that I was given when I had gone to visit a church administrator rather early in the morning. The receptionist said to me, "You will please wait about twenty minutes, the pastor is now reading his Bible."

It appears that fixed hours for counseling have to be set so that the congregation may know for certain at what hours the pastor can be reached. The fact that a member of the church knows that he could, if he so chose, see his pastor or youth leader at five o'clock this afternoon goes a long way toward overcoming a feeling of exclusion. The times for counseling sessions often are set with little regard for the situation of a congregation of working people. The hours between 10 and 12 in the morning are feasible only for the smallest fraction of the members. The hours must be suitable for people engaged in occupations. This will be the case between 5 and 7 o'clock in the evening. And it should further be possible to have definite appointments between 8 and 10 o'clock at night. Moreover, and this should be indicated on the schedule at the door, appointments may be made by telephone for any other hour, be that with the pastor or with other church workers. Withal, accommodations will have to be made to situations. It is no small matter when an overworked man of the church is asked and he says, "Yes, surely, you may come at 11 o'clock tonight." But what an experience when the inquirer sees the coffee pot on the table and cigarettes there too and the first statement he hears is, "So, my friend, now we have time to drink coffee till morning." That is true pastoral concern.

It need not be said that such demands must not be hardened into rules. It is natural that we avoid patterns on this score. But the possibility for such procedure must be granted. The case of the medical student is comparable. As soon as he has completed his preliminary examination he learns never to go out during the evening without leaving an address at which he may be reached. This should apply equally to the pastor. It is possible that one of us may not have a night's rest interrupted throughout his career by a call to pray with a dying person or to administer the Sacrament to him. Yet, how irresponsible it is when a pastor cannot be reached for such an emergency. When a congregation knows that such seemingly small details are not left to chance but are regulated no less than the cash-account in the safe, the preparation of the sermon at the desk, and the daily prayer (let the order of listing be noted), there can be such a thing as atmosphere conducive to pastoral care.

The visitor who comes for an hour of counseling will be shown to a waiting room, if possible, without being plied with questions. The pastor comes out of his office and invites the visitor to come with him. Rumor has it that in many places it still happens that a bass voice will roar, "Next, please!" which shatters that special thing we call conducive atmosphere. The pastor's office may be very small, but it can be too large. Walking from the entrance to the chair at the desk behind which the mighty man enveloped in cigar smoke sits enthroned can be gruesome torture for a girl who is expecting a child and is not married. As was described in the chapter on counseling, it is usually the pastor's duty to open the session. This he may do by alluding to an incident known to both participants or by calmly asking whether and how he may be helpful.

We are now interested in the place for counseling. The need for the counselee to be deliberative causes him to direct his eyes toward some point in the room. The more earnest and weighty the matter is, the less likely the participants are to look at each other. Thus the choice of pictures for the pastor's study can be very meaningful. Neither the still life drawing by aunt Frieda nor a landscape will be appropriate to the needs of the eye that anxiously casts about for an object that will inspire calmness and security.

The symbolical force of pictures can be decisive. A representation of the archangel Michael who slays the dragon with the deft gesture of one who has his repose in God can be a symbol of one's own combat as a Michael. It is not only the person in the care of the pastor but also the pastor himself who needs a point at which to fix his gaze so that he may relax to recover strength and, primarily, to be prepared for the temptation of the devil that is so often and variously posed in pastoral counseling. For him a picture of the suffering Christ will serve well; he is in the service of Christ and counts on Christ's forgiveness as he conducts his spiritual office. It can be a picture of a burning candle that pierces the darkness with its light and dispenses warmth as it uses itself up. In any case, these studiously chosen pictures can provide the help that both counselee and counselor require.

There is also some question as to whether or not there should be a desk or table between the partners to the counseling. In many cases the desk is a hindrance. In other instances it may prove to be a saving island. The best answer seems to be a comfortable chair set conveniently to the side of the desk where it is possible for the counselee to look past the pastor. However, he should not be made to look out a window nor should it be into the garish light of the sun.

Sudden interruption is the death of a session in counseling. In the age of the telephone it is hard to avoid this. But occasionally the pastor should make use of the beneficent arrangement by which the telephone operator disconnects the telephone for a while and reports later the names or numbers of people who may have tried to call in. A button that lights a lamp outside the study and signals that there must be no admittance for the time being is simple to install and serves well. By it the pastor's wife, children, and secretary know that they must by all means keep out. It can be helpful to make the visitor aware of this arrangement. All necessary papers, seals, and the like should be ready at hand. It will not do ever and again to interrupt a simple counseling session of some technical character by having the pastor jump up and go hunting.

In order that the pastor's study may be appointed as a place of worship there must be a fixed place for prayer. This calls for a private altar. To reject this piece of furniture as an evidence of a Catholicizing trend reveals a lack of understanding of what it means in an evangelical sense to speak of a "place of prayer." The same applies here that has been said about the altar in the church. But if this altar is an ornamental piece only or an object on which the pastor exercises his archeological and liturgical bent, then it becomes an altar of Baal. Let the altar be something more than a place with an open Bible and a candle that burns because it is molded of pure beeswax and is a worthy adornment for such a place. Let pastor and counselee occasionally pray together there, and that altar will become the source of new spiritual strength. Before this altar the pastor begins his work for the day, and there he concludes it at night. Before it he begins his meditation on the text for his sermon, and before it he pauses as he goes into the sacristy. To be sure, all this can happen at his desk. But there are those among us who by their faith in the incarnation deny that the only possibility for prayer is in the midst of ashtrays, newly arrived correspondence, and records of financial transactions in the parish.

We have already treated of the sacristy as place for private confession. We may now repeat what was stated in the section on confession and point out that the pastor's office and the room for private confession are on principle not the same. It may be granted that the atmosphere in the room for confession is supported by the same loving concern and serves the same purpose that pervades all pastoral guidance. But the element of liturgical strictness that is to prevail in the room for confession is not repulsive but a positive aid.

Even as pastoral counseling and confession are distinguished basically by differing content and objectives, so the objective happening of proclaimed grace will have to be made more evident by the very appointments of the room for confession. Thus the sacristy used as a room for confession will require little more than an altar. Central to the view of the person confessing will be the cross, which will also indicate the direction in which the father confessor is to look. Anything additional may distract.

Confession is not a comfortable affair. It comes not at the beginning but at the culmination of a pastoral relationship. It must therefore do without the aids that a visitor may need in the counseling room. Usually, the course runs from the counseling room to the room for confession. The sacristy, also, must not be too large. Under all circumstances, disturbances must be made impossible. Even so—and let this be asserted with good reason—the pastor must not lock himself in with his visitor, be that in the room for counseling or for confession.

Whoever concerns himself with rooms for pastoral purposes will in a special measure have to deal with the question of whether and to what extent he ought to use psychological insights. If this is done for the sake of technique, the pastor is likely to go out of bounds, and the good pastor will become a bad psychotherapist. But if this is done out of love for the person entrusted to him for pastoral care, it will be necessary to give serious thought to what most physicians, nurses, and lawyers consider self-evident.[3]

PART IV

*The
Time When
We Proclaim*

INCARNATION INVOLVES TIME

Time is just as much a part of the dealings of God with the world as is place. The incarnation is tied to a *kairos* of God as well as to place. "It came to pass when . . ." is an extension of the *kairos* of creation which in the Book of Genesis determines the acts of God. You see, the Word of God occurs not only in space but also in time. There is a rhythm in which all creaturely life runs its course, and this rhythm is determinative for God's action in the world. Space and time are not entities that are only of philosophical perception, as Kant and Heidegger said; they stand in relationship to the creation and redemption of the world. There is neither nonhistoricity of the *logos* nor timelessness of the *logos*. As long as this eon shall last, it will be under the law of time. Cabala turns about the mystery of time, and time is seen as the background of number.[1]

It is from the concept of time that numbers get their value. Number is definition and demonstration of the infinite.[2] Time is the possibility of arresting infinite things for finitude with such means as are at our command. Thus, wherever time is ignored as a determining factor, a fact of God's creation is overlooked. "When the fullness of time was come," God's revelation took place.

The numbers given us in the Bible, and whose meaning are still concealed from us, enable us to discern that God is not only Lord of space but also of the concept of time. The Revelation of St. John clearly speaks of a time or of two or more times. Also in the Bible *kairos* is not simply time but rather the definite point of time at which something happens. Thus the deeds of God are not done arbitrarily and independently of time. God performs his will at a time and moment foreseen by him.

From this we shall probably have to learn anew something about our own lives; namely that what our hands are given to do by God's command is bound up with a right time for doing it. In order that a thing may be said in the right way, it must be said at the right time. And we are not so disposed that we can at all times perceive in the same way. There is a variation in periods of time. In them we can easily discern up and down movements and also a circular movement. These variations we call rhythms. This rhythm of God moves, from its start in creation, through all manifestations of life in the creature world. It rises to a crowning and keystone rhythm in the relationship of Christmas, Good Friday and Easter to each other.

The course of the individual human life is imbedded in this rhythm. This life, as we have shown in Part I, makes its rhythmic turn in old age back to the rhythm of the child. The rhythm of life from conception through birth, zenith, decline, and death accords with the rhythm of sunrise, noon, twilight, and night. As long as the world shall have to wait for the return of Christ, so long this rhythm will continue (Genesis 8). Only harm can result if this God-willed law of cosmic rhythm is overlooked, ignored, or even consciously violated. Proof of this can easily be given from findings in neurology and from research in internal medicine.

A further example is the day of rest. The benefits of it are not received on some free day at whatever time. The fact is that, in the long run, harm comes when a day other than the seventh day is set aside for rest. In Russia the ten-day workweek has been abolished. The motivation for this was given by the physicians. They could prove that the efficiency of a workman—and this is what counts in Russia—is reduced when the rhythm of the seventh day for rest is interrupted.

Developmental psychology proceeds on the basis of seven-year stages in a human being's development, and it can ascertain basic psychological and organic changes for the 7-14-21-year periods. It is exactly the interruption of this rhythm at the given stage of development in young people that is causing us so much trouble in our Western culture.

Or take the adults. It is no mere guesswork when we insist that they should have at least seven hours of sleep. To this someone could add a word on the seven stages of meditation; yet another may want to show how the number three in the Trinity can be added to the four of the primal elements. By putting all this together one may in some measure sense the rhythmic feature that is hidden in God's order of creation. We do not mind being called modern Gnostics because we think that the basic laws of cosmic living cannot only be rationally perceived but that in them we can also see the mysteries of God reflected as they pervade all creaturely life.

Marginally let it be noted that in astronomy the number seven, the number groupings of three plus four and of three times four, dominates the cosmic courses. As long as these insights are divorced from the fact that Christ is the fulfiller of the law (but not its destroyer), this rhythm of the number can quickly become atheistic magic. But when the event of Christ is taken to be a fulfillment of and key to the hidden laws of nature, then we can see and employ this rhythm as an aid in service to the world.[3] To this end we shall have to place the calendar year and the church year in relationship to each other. Similarly, we shall have to place the rhythm of life and the rhythm of the day in reference to each other.[4]

But it will also be necessary to recognize that besides time there is also inopportune time. Little thought has been given to this. It is recognized that precisely in the life of faith the concept of the right moment does have decisive significance. It is an experience of all spiritual living that we must recognize the need of going through deep valleys of inopportune time in order to scale the heights of *kairos,* and that we must directly descend again in order to conquer those heights once more. The rhythm in the life of the believer is comparable to the rhythm of the wave. The church has been represented symbolically as a ship upon the waves. As one meditates on this he may have an experience of the laws of opportune and inopportune time in spiritual living

RHYTHM IN NATURE
AND IN THE CHURCH YEAR

As he celebrates the liturgy on the eve of Easter the priest of the Orthodox Church proclaims the glad tidings of the resurrection of Christ. As he does this he stands before the entrance to the church and turns to face in the four directions of the compass, also upward and downward. This action is to show that the resurrection is of consequence for man and for the whole of creation.

The ancient church had a profound understanding of this. The early Christians deemed the happenings in nature to be consequences of the Christ event. They did not regulate the rhythm of week and year by the season but by events of salvation manifested in Christ. Evidence of this shows up first in the replacement of the Jewish Sabbath with Sunday as the holy day of the week for the Christian congregation. The Epistle of Barnabas states in 15:8, "The Sabbath that we now observe does not please me. But I am pleased with the one that I have made. When I shall have brought all things to rest, I will make the beginning of an eighth day. That will be the beginning of another world. Therefore we joyfully celebrate the eighth day. It is the day on which Jesus arose from the dead."

According to the tradition of the ancient church, the outpouring of the Holy Spirit also took place on the Lord's Day. The first to use this fact as he set forth the meaning of Pentecost was Isidore of Seville.[5]

If we want to see how far the proclamation and liturgy of our time are removed from such thinking, we need but call to mind the

181

substance of Easter sermons at the turn of the century. They interpreted the Christ event as the consequence of cosmic events. This probably is still so in some instances. The ancient church had it this way: events in nature are evidence of Christ's rulership over the cosmos. More recently preachers have regarded Easter as the resurrection of nature and Christmas as the start of the sun's ascent over the equator.

For us right now and for our proclamation there is a further danger, namely that no connection at all is seen between God's acts of salvation in Christ and the run of events in the cosmos. This means that we lose sight of Christ as the *pantocrator*. The result can be that we fall victim to the hidden powers of nature, because our liturgical celebrations can no longer show the dependence of cosmic events on the salvatory work of Christ. It is not because nature then renews itself that Easter comes in the springtime, but the renewal of nature is possible only because of the resurrection of him who is the Lord of all worlds. Indeed, nature ran its courses in the ages before Christ; but the deep significance of this comes to light only when the mere myth of the dying and reviving god is displaced by the reality of God in Jesus Christ. From Krishna to Balder we have only myth. From the cross to Easter Day we have meaning that makes all natural events meaningful.

The reckoning of time that begins with the birth of Jesus Christ is not a trick in figures to simplify the teaching of history. For that purpose it is, historically speaking, too incorrect. Much rather does it serve to show that Jesus Christ is the anchor point in history, the turning point from darkness to light, from myth to revelation. All this contributes to the need for an order of the church year that is something more than an agenda which pastor and people may change according to whim. This order is an aid to enfolding the Christ event in the totality of man's being as the successive seasons of the year run their courses. The natural run of cosmic events affords a God-given opportunity to make visible, at the hand of the Word of God, the deed of God for the children of men.

It is from this position that the other festival seasons also take their meaning. Take Epiphanytide. If it is taken to be only a transition from Christmas to Passiontide and used merely to make the proclamation of Christmas more emphatic, then it will be less possible to bring home to the congregation the force of the Passion event. Epiphany does not center in the appearance of the star, and certainly not in the coming of the wise men. What "appears" in this season is the fullness of the power of Christ as *pantocrator* who lies in the manger as a helpless child. The star shines in his service as it points the way. Before him wisdom pays its respects. Epiphany discloses how natural events and human wisdom must gravitate toward the Child in the manger. At the beginning of the way that God takes through the world all powers and forces of the earth stand ready to be employed in his service. This is witness to the kingdom of God that is veiled in the manger.

From this witness the way goes through the old line Epistle and Gospel lessons to pre-Lent. These lessons unfold this kingdom as the lordship of Christ over the raging sea, over sickness and death (the stilling of the storm, the healing of the demon-possessed, the raising of the youth at Nain). But this Lord suffers and dies for the sake of every single human being. The boundless love of God for us, his children, can be made truly emphatic in the Pre-Lenten and Lenten seasons only when the lordship and glory of him whom wind and wave obey have already been seen. He who washes men's feet is no less than the Lord of sickness. He whose robe occasions casting of lots for possession of it is also the one to whom the wise men of the world pay homage. This is how Epiphanytide and Passiontide are closely related to each other.[6]

It is not by chance that the Bible's account of the crucifixion sets the darkness of men's sin and the darkening of the sun side by side. On this passage of Scripture all attempts at demythologizing utterly fail to bring out the deeper relationships with which the Bible is concerned, whether the attempts be exegetically in order or not. The question whether the notice about the darkened sun is a mythological overlay or a fact that can be verified by astronomy is not an essential question. The decisive thing is that the notice stands there and that it says something about the dominion of the crucified Christ over mankind *and* over the cosmos. It simply will not do to consider as incidental inserts the many references in the Bible to the relationship of events in nature to salvatory events. These references are nothing less than aids in pastoral care. They help to disclose the deep meaning in the fact that he who is the ruling servant of God is also the suffering servant.

Similarly, the liturgical colors of the church year can be aids in pastoral care. The two hues of violet show that there can be joy and earnestness at the same time. When the confirmands are asked the meaning of violet, they sometimes answer, "Lilac is neither a whole nor a half." This means exactly what Advent is to convey: earnestness, preparation, and joyous thanksgiving. The hymns of Advent have it the same.

But then, when white gleams from pulpit and altar, dawn yields to the sun and the same message is found in our hymns. Take Kasper Friedrich Nachtenhoefer's sun of Christmas, or Paul Gerhardt's hero who strides forth from his chamber; these are signs of a breakthrough—darkness gives way to brightly shining light.

Then there is the pre-Lenten season. Already in pre-Christian times it was seen as betokening joyous hope. The *Edda* attests to this. When used during the pre-Lenten season, green bespeaks hope that looks forward to the cross and resurrection of Christ by which his hidden kingship will be veiled today and tomorrow revealed to all.

Black, however, is the color of negation. The sense of it applies only to Good Friday. Here we have the absolute end. Here everything is really finished. At this point Protestant theology must be ever so thankful to Bultmann, because he has worked out the absolute "finish" so definitely that there can be no mistaking it.

The white of Thursday in Holy Week plants the dialectic of Holy Scripture right in the middle of the Week for eyes to see. Life and death, sin and grace, promise and judgment, Thursday and cross, white and black. This again is an aid in soul-care. The congregation is prompted to feel the tension of Holy Week.

But this aid stands idle unless it is recognized that the rhythm of color and the rhythm of the cosmos stand in the service of God as he acts for our good. This should be most clearly felt in the service of worship on Saturday in Holy Week. Between the darkness of the ninth hour and "very early on the first day of the week" a mysterious silence hovers over Saturday. It shows us the earth in revolt (Matthew 28:2). The sinister forces of the cosmos surge angrily against God's victory in the depths of men's hearts. When the organ falls silent and the candles are snuffed out, only to come to singing, shining life again with the proclamation of the jubilant Easter message—ah, but something more happens here than when discussion is held about the tomb, whether it was empty or not.

After this comes the rhythm of the 40 days to the Ascension of our Lord. This span of time can be understood only in reference to the 40 days and nights of fasting that Jesus spent in the wilderness, or to the fasting of Moses at Sinai, or to Elijah who by the power and providence of God was brought to Horeb (Matthew 4:2; Exodus 34:28; 1 Kings 19:8). Parallel with and in contrast to these earlier periods, these 40 days are a time of rejoicing. The wedding guests cannot fast so long as the Bridegroom is among them. In the manner of a profound dialectic there is simultaneously in these 40 days a "coming to rest" in the midst of exciting joy, jubilation, and certainty after the revolutionary events between Palm Sunday and Easter. There probably is not a single preacher left in our church who proclaims to his congregation the event of the ascension in terms of a specific place. And there likely are not too many among us who can make plain to the congregation out of the recurring 40-day rhythm the completed circle of "from the Father—to the Father." Rhythm of the church year, and the possibilities of it in the care of souls—see how it recommends itself.

Pentecost, we know, stood in relationship to one of the harvest festivals of Israel. Relatively little is known about the original fixing of the date for its observance. However, the ancient liturgies indicate that the harvest on the fields was related to a world become ripe for the harvest and that the Holy Spirit had made reapers ready for the harvest. The reaping can now take place. The world that has been made ready for the harvest by Golgotha and Easter has become the field for the lordship of Christ. The red color that on this birthday of the church reminds of the blood of the martyrs and of the fire of the Holy Spirit also points to seed and harvest. Although the Roman Church asserts with some hesitancy that "the blood of the martyrs is the seed of the church," there is in that statement symbolism of events in nature for events in the history of salvation.

In face of all this, certain difficulties must be taken into account. One of these is the duration of the rhythm and whether it should be of 40 or 60 days. There are the various fixed days on which the Nativity is celebrated. It was out of missionary considerations that this festival was placed where we now have it in the West. Advisedly, therefore, we have not mentioned the apparent parallel between the return of the sunlight and the festival of Christ's birth. By how much the later developments in church history contradict the relationships just now pointed out is not a question that can be thoroughly answered. Whatever this may mean, we hold to the connection between events of salvation and events in nature as Scripture has it, between the symbolism of color and the Christian festivals; and we hold to the ever recurring relationship between concepts of time that have firm significance in the Bible (rhythm of creation, 40-day rhythm) and the events of salvation in the New Testament.

The *kairos* of God is not seen in the events of nature by themselves. Apart from the Bible's witness to Christ, the rhythm of nature is reduced to a kind of magic. Cognizance must be taken of the relationship to each other of the rhythms of nature and the events of salvation. If this is not done, we are robbed of a God-given opportunity for good in pastoral care; namely, to have the totality of man permeated by the totality of Christ as *pantocrator*. Even so, the human being will move along in the rhythm of the church year only when the church's message is addressed to the totality of man in *martyria*, *diakonia*, and *leitourgia*.

RHYTHM OF LIFE
AND OF THE DAY (THE HOURS)

The Rule of the Benedictines prescribes Hours in the rhythm of seven as in creation.[7] The scriptural basis for this is Psalm 119: 164, "Seven times a day I praise thee." The specific times for prayer are the first, third, sixth, and ninth hours plus the time for Vespers and for Compline. It is a known fact that the custom of assigning prayer to definite times of the day is not peculiar to the Christian community. The synagogue has hours of prayer. These are at the third, sixth, and ninth hours, even as these times are repeatedly mentioned in the Acts of the Apostles. In all likelihood these are the roots of the later monastical Hours.

Practically all religions have hours of prayer stipulated for days which are not the day for the main period of worship. This fact takes us to the close connection that obtains between natural event and prayer. The relation between natural year and church year has a parallel in the connection between the course of a day and hours of prayer.

When we consider the monastical Hours, we can easily discern a harking back to the Psalms. It cannot be proved definitely that a specific selection of Psalms was prayed at definite hours in the synagogue service. It cannot be denied, however, that the praying of Psalms was connected with the course of the day in a special way. Psalm 119:62 speaks of a man arising at midnight to praise his God. In Psalm 134 we learn of servants of God who stand in the Temple in the night. We hear of the blending of the sun's light

187

with the glory of God. The thought of continuous prayer runs quite noticeably through the Psalms. For our present purpose it is quite essential to inquire into the character of the various times of the day to which suitable forms of prayer are related.

We begin with Vigil, the nocturnal prayer, because we know with reasonable certainty that it was prayed in the Temple and also in the ancient church. *Vigilia* means watch in the night and is taken from the language of Roman soldiers. The concept has been modulated to have the general meaning of watchfulness and preparedness for what is to come. That is why there are two lines of thought in the church's Prayer of Vigil: (1) Petition for safekeeping in the dark, and (2) Thanks for the certainty of the coming light, coupled with the petition for readiness to act in that light.

In the Roman Church Compline was orginally the prayer for the night. The liturgical movement of our church has again taken the two indicated lines of thought as belonging to Compline. By itself Compline is the prayer before going to bed late at night, and it cannot be taken as Lauds, the prayer of praise at dawn, nor as Vespers. Night is the time of the oppressive powers. This is age-old human understanding. Night is that part of the day when darkness threatens and in which our adversary "prowls around like a roaring lion." In order to demonstrate that the preserving power of God is particularly needed in the night hours we need only to point out what burdens fall to sensitive or depressed persons in the night.

This is the reason why Psalms 4, 91, and 134 are the anciently prescribed Psalms for Compline. They are knit together by the related assertions they contain: of distress (4), of trust in God's protection (91), and of fellowship with those who in the night watch before the throne of grace in behalf of others (134). This triad also indicates what is the true concern in Compline.

Tersteegen, counting himself as one of those who cannot sleep in the night, expresses out of deep insight what they have in common, "Now is the time to sleep, but let him who cannot sleep join me in adoration." To sleep in the night is the normal thing. But great is the number of those who are sleepless. Any one of them can be lifted out of gloomy ponderings and despair by his awareness of his fellowship with those who wake ". . . let him who cannot sleep adore with me." No longer, then, are they in the fellowship of those who despair; they are in the fellowship of those who worship. From this vantage point Psalm 134 becomes transparent. "Come, bless the Lord, all you servants of the Lord, who stand by night in the house of the Lord!"

There is a definite advantage for the sick person to know about this fellowship of those who wake in the night and adore. It should be pointed out to him. For him as for others the night is a time of being misled, of despairing. Downright evil thoughts come to us. The hymn for Compline speaks of these. *Treib weg die Träum, so schädlich sein, dazu nächtlich Phantasein. Den Feind verjag, das unser Leib in deinem Schutze reine bleib."* (Dispel the dreams that harm, and the gruesome fantasy. Drive the foe away, so that our bodies may be kept whole by your protection.) This is reason why the meditative permeation of the word for dying in Psalm 31:5 has a proper place in Compline. The Lord gave up his spirit in the hour of the darkness of death; therefore it is possible for us to endure and persevere through the night with this his prayer, even when we are caught up in the depths of night and death.

From Compline we go to Lauds and Matins. These are really the songs of praise for the morning. "Therefore let us not sleep, as do others; but let us watch and be sober" (1 Thess. 5:6). This is the tenor of these morning prayers. We do not carry the gloomy ponderings of the night into the day. With the new day life begins afresh. With the beginning of every day there comes a suggestion of the dawn of the first day. By the grace of God we may put away what makes us slothful. One may feel that it is futile to go onto the same old treadmill of workday life, but this feeling is transmuted to the motivation with which each day should be met: "And my mouth shall show forth thy praise" (Psalm 51:15).

Lectures on occupational motivation and psychotherapeutic teachings about sublimation, of which we have a surplus, must take second place when the morning prayer of the church has shed its light on the meaning of the new day. Meditative prayer touches the deeper layers of man's being, where rational consciousness does not operate with "Yes, but . . ."

In *The Benedictus*, which is the original Psalm of the morning prayer, the all-embracing reason why a man owes praise to God at the beginning of the day is given: "For he has visited and redeemed his people." This is how you begin the day at God's hand. This is how you may have the confidence that this day, no matter what it may bring, stands under the promise of God, "Through the tender mercy of our God, when the day shall dawn upon us from on high" (Luke 1:78).

When the sun is at its zenith, the work of the day has also come to its high point. It seems strange to the bewildered men of our time that the church should ring the bell for prayer at noon. To a commendable extent we have rediscovered Matins and Vespers for our workdays and conferences. Midday prayer, however, does not yet occur to us. This prayer is quite distinct from prayer at mealtime. It is not a prayer of thanks for the renewed gift of food; it is rather a special way of praising God for standing eternally at the zenith of his power. Even as Paul Gerhardt likens the sun to Jesus Christ, *Die Sonne, die mir lachet* (The sun that smiles upon me), so noonday prayer begins with the words of praise, "Now to the King eternal, immortal, invisible, the only wise God, be honor and glory for ever and ever. Amen" (1 Tim. 1:17). Psalm 36:6-10 goes on with this same praise. The goodness of God really does "extend to the heavens."

Of course, there is interruption of the day's work by the congregation's praise at noon. But this teaches us something. It is not work that gives meaning to life but he who commends work to us. Tradition of the ancient church has it that the archangel Gabriel made his annunciation in the noonhour.

It is not only in Catholic communities that the ringing of the church bell at noon is called *Angelus Dei.*

According to legend, it was at noon that the angel of the Lord delivered his message. The divine event at Bethlehem marked high noon for the world, the breaking in of endtime under the sun of God. This is the thought by which parts of Luke 1 and John 1 are given place in the prayer at noon.

Rest in the middle of work is an aid in soul-care. One must really have experienced this in order to be convinced of it and to recommend it to others convincingly. He can feel it in his bones if he will join those in southern lands who escape the heat of the day by resting in the cool of the church building even as the church commends them to do.

The Hour that has persisted most in evangelical Christendom is Vespers. One may observe how it serves far and wide as the pause that separates workday from the period of rest at evening. To be sure, the vesper bell usually signals the rest period in the ears and minds of our congregations, yet the relaxation that is felt then is a carry-over of aid from Vespers which has come to every individual in the nation through the centuries.

In her wisdom the church has provided a prayer for the evening in which a large place is given to personal intercession. Generally, we now engage in prayer just before we go to sleep. In our pastoral contacts we hear the constant complaint that then, even with the best of intention, prayer is either forgotten or that concentration of thought is very difficult. These people seem to have forgotten that the church has prepared a prayer for the time immediately before the night's rest, and in the monastical form of that prayer has provided ample quiet time for personal concerns in this vesper prayer. In the interest of spiritual well-being the recommendation will have to be made ever and again that the members of the congregation learn anew not to postpone their evening prayers to the moment at which they go to sleep. There are other good possibilities: the last ten minutes at the desk, a short period before the evening meal, a time of spiritual relaxation and collecting of thoughts directly after dinner. With good purpose men of every occupation can more easily make use of a few minutes at these times for vesper-prayer than at the time before going to sleep, when spiritual concentration is not so easy.

The petition of Psalm 106, which runs through all the Hours, is taken up once more: that God by his grace may remember us. Psalm 69 continues the petition that God would hear us. The focus of Vespers, however, according to ancient usage, is on the Magnificat as praise for the grace which God has granted on another day. Since Mary's song of praise includes both isolation and premonition of suffering, the Magnificat can give comfort particularly when it is prayed at the end of a day when the mercy of God appears not to have endured "from generation to generation," not to have "put down the mighty from their thrones," not to have "filled the hungry with good things." There is nightfall, and there is the step into the dark, but up front stands the jubilant certainty that God has "regarded the low estate of his handmaiden." The monastical conclusion, "The almighty, gracious God grant us a peaceful night and a holy end" again leads to the parallel between the end of day, the end of life, and the end of the world.

Thus there is fulfilled in the vesper prayer the sense of the Hours through the day. It sums up what has been, and it prepares for what is to come. In the vesper-prayer, at the hour when the sun sets only to appear again on the morrow, recognition is made of the God who has no beginning and no ending.

Martin Luther, with some show of reason, gives a kind of directive in the *Small Catechism* for hours of prayer and has them only for morning and evening.[8] Anyone that knows the text of the Hours will at once notice that both of Martin Luther's prayers are oriented by them, even to linguistic formulation. The opening sentence is there, "In the name of the Father, and of the Son, and of the Holy Spirit." The reference to Psalm 31:5 is there, as this is known to us in Compline. And the invoking of the protection against the wicked enemy is there. For our present purpose the closing sentence in Luther's evening prayer is of especial importance, the sentence which he placed after the "Amen," "Then you should go to sleep immediately and joyfully." From this it is irrefutably clear that the much tried Luther knew of the therapeutic value of regular prayer. For such joyous sleeping is conceivable only after petition for protection against the evil powers. In his morning prayer reference is also made to the "danger and harm" that lurk in the dark of night, and commendation is made to the guardian angel "that the wicked one have no power over me."

Luther himself observed the Order of the Hours even though he did not expressly make it mandatory for his congregation. One must remember that in the time of the Reformation this Order of the Hours was counted among the practices that were neither expressly forbidden nor commanded. Wherever in Luther's thinking such an order turned out to be monkery, that is, served as a way of

storing up merit by works through fulfillment of a prayer duty, it
was emphatically put aside.

To be sure, this same danger does not threaten today. Because the
Hours have fallen into disuse, our congregations feel a need which
can be satisfied in no other way. Every one of us knows, of course,
how the rhythm of work during the day has made the ancient Hours
quite impracticable. This does not mean, however, that the whole
matter should be skipped. Even though in modern industrial life
the threefold hour of Psalm-prayer and praise cannot be held, surely
it would still be possible to observe the *kairos* of a minute for prayer.
This, however, requires two new insights: the rediscovery of the
fixed form of prayer, and the necessity of having a definite time and
place for the entire Hour in which intercession is made for and in
fellowship with those who may have only thirty seconds for the
same purpose.

As so often in the history of Protestant liturgical practice, it was
misuse that caused the demise of set forms of prayer. When the sup-
porting strengths of Pietism waned, there remained hardly a trace
of the wave of free prayer, which had been derived from formulated
prayer, as church history will show. That is how we came by the
impoverishment in prayer which still prevails. After World War I
we were favored with formulated prayers again, prayers that are
not cast in language of the past and yet are not as flat as everyday
speech.[9] It is significant that fixed forms of prayer and timely hymns
were recovered at about the same time. If there can be no ranking
of the primary and secondary here, mention can be made of mutual
interaction between the two.

There is only one place outside the service of worship at which
we have not lost the formulated prayer, namely in prayers for children. A far larger number of persons than we surmise must live
on the treasure of prayer that is made up of verses for children.
This has been proved by war and imprisonment. When Psalm-
prayers ceased to be a substantial part of public worship, formulated
prayer also practically ceased to be a possession of the Christian.
Now we see people go into the hour of death lacking the riches
of formulated prayer which the church should have given them in
catechetical instruction. In his hour of death our Lord prayed

194 THE TIME WHEN WE PROCLAIM

from a Psalm. Free prayer is impossible for a person who is critically ill, or dying, or severely depressed, or deeply disturbed. This is the reason why it is of great importance, in the interest of pastoral care, that there be a recovery of formulated prayer, both as Psalm-prayer and as regular church prayer, and this in language that is genuinely of our day.

In the school of prayer free prayers have their proper place in the upper grades. Prayer of fixed form serves to guide and to enrich, even as formal liturgy does. The principle of the ancient church *"lex credendi—lex orandi"* can be considered and put into practice anew in reference to formulated prayer.

The places at which small fellowship groups gather at a definite hour for regular prayer are spiritual wellsprings for their environment. It has been demonstrated particularly in recent years how effectively we can bridge space and time with intercessory prayer. It will not do to exhort modern man to a life of prayer unless he knows that there are others praying for him. Individuals must know that prayer is made for them in regular hours of prayer even when they themselves are hindered from prayer, be they workers in the factory, mothers with their children, or even overworked clergymen. Most of us have experienced in recent years that streams of strength flow from regular intercessory prayer. So long as we cannot tell a man when, where, and in what words his church has stood by him in his needs and joys, we cannot commend his church to him as his church home.

Rhythm of the day and rhythm of prayer lend meaning to each other. Similarly, there is interplay between liturgical order and divinely ordained fellowship. Even as morning, noon, and night are given meaning by prayer, so activities in the rhythm of the day have their quality determined by the *oratio continua* (prayer without ceasing)—and this not by force of rules. It is all of brotherly kindness.

DIE UNZEIT

Emil Brunner has called attention to the fact that in the German language it is possible to form the word *Unmensch* and thus express a perversion in man which makes him the opposite of what he ought to be.[10] Brunner goes on to show that the opposite of the horse's nature cannot be rendered by *Unpferd*. And the combination *Untier* plainly does not yield the sense of perversion but simply characterizes the beast as of unusually large size. It is of interest also to note that we cannot speak of *Unraum* in contrast to space; but we can speak of *Unzeit* in contrast to time. Holy Scriptures can say, "My time is in thy hands." But one would hardly say, My space is in your hands. Time, then, is a concept that intrinsically may have positive and negative valuation. All this leads up to the point that there can be *Unzeit* in spiritual life.

In the New Testament, times of overt activity are always followed by times of quiet contemplation—this at the behest of Jesus. If spiritual living is to move along with God's time, there will have to be hours of going-into-the desert. To "go into the desert" means, on the one hand, to be alone in order to meet and to combat the powers; and, on the other hand, it means to prepare for new undertakings. In our life of faith we have periods of dryness. A pastor will often have such periods in counseling. Now, as in the past, a man can get into the distress of not being able to pray. He has times when he is especially under the stress of temptation. Or he may simply be obtuse when spiritual questions are posed to him.

195

Take for example the time of Samuel. The voice of prophecy was seldom heard in his day. There was Eli. Experienced in spiritual matters as he was, he did not discern that the voice which wakened Samuel from sleep was the voice of the Lord. This means that *Unzeit* in spiritual living can last a long time.

If our time is a time in which the spiritual powers of healing and of genuine prophecy fail, does it not bear the stamp of *Unzeit?* In all humility we dare to ask: Have the last twenty years not turned up some evidence that a period of spiritual *Unzeit* is about to pass over? It seems to us that a closer look indicates that the pessimistic view that our time is an era of godless materialism is not tenable.

It will have to be said that pastoral counsel is required even in *Unzeit*. This is not self-evident. We can so easily veer toward the erroneous opinion that we might grant or prescribe for those in our care some sort of spiritual fasting. But it is just as true that we must not make demands of *Unzeit* that can be fulfilled only at the right time. Exhortations to the effect that you must pray or that you must count wholly on Jesus Christ not only come close to being empty words, but they are of no effect because no account is taken in them of the nature of *Unzeit*.

The one consoling fact during *Unzeit* is that we live in the fellowship of the Third Article. If one is incapable of saying free prayer, then he who is in our care must know, that is he must be expressly told, that he is carried along on the prayers of others. Never, no never must the idea be fostered that the rhythm of prayer may be broken. By the sacramental character of the Word, with its promise of efficacy, much more happens in every prayer session than can be consciously grasped with the mind. The objection which could be raised that this ascribes a certain magical element to the Word can be directly answered with the admonition that is given repeatedly in the New Testament to continue in prayer, to "pray without ceasing." This last advice was not given by a man who strode through life without being tempted in any way. It was given by the Apostle Paul. He conceded even after his hour of conversion that he had not already attained and that he continued to live by the law of doing that evil which he did not will to do.

As practicing Christians we must not let the vocabulary of God's language go to sleep. Experience in spiritual living does not show that you can again pick up the broken relationship with God as whim and mood may direct. Precisely in *Unzeit* it is high time to point out that formulated prayer is of great importance, as is participation in the life of the congregation.

One of the difficult problems in the present theological situation comes with the division of opinion on fellowship in the Lord's Supper. Quite often eucharistic fasting is recommended as a solution. This recommendation is given on the assumption that pertinent spiritual insights may thus be gained. It is true that, by grace, proper fasting can lead to spiritual experiences. But wherever there has been fasting in the church to combat *Unzeit,* the only sustenance received at all was by the Lord's Supper. We shall therefore not take sides with the advocates of eucharistic fasting as a way of achieving consensus in the question of altar fellowship. This does not mean to imply that mere togetherness in celebrating the Sacrament makes for fellowship in the Sacrament. Anyone who would claim this does not understand the tension that exists in the New Testament between truth and love. In every instance in which *Unzeit,* with its spiritual void, is felt to be oppressive and distressing, the advice may be given that the Sacrament be used. However, if the condition is not experienced as distressing but taken to be a continuing thing which one does not even *want* to change, then the person should be warned against use of the Sacrament. According to the confessions, the gift of the Holy Supper is not diminished even when an evil man administers it or a knave receives it.[11]

On the other hand, it must be said with equal earnestness that one makes himself guilty of the Sacrament if he receives it for a reason other than to satisfy his spiritual hunger. Wherever in pastoral duties we meet with *Unzeit* as a spiritual void we gain nothing in the conquest of it by relinquishing our arms so soon and by withdrawing the last of the sentries that still stand guard.

There is, moreover, such a thing as *Unzeit* in the midst of what purports to be spiritual activities. We refer to the well-nigh unbearable stupidity of the agendas for the days of our conferences and meetings. Breakfast at 8; Bible study from 9 to 10 o'clock, with summary and address following; supper at 7, and evening devotions at 8:45. By the way, there follows what is not noted in the agenda: jesting in the dormitory about salaries—how the church leaders have put them up or down. Unless we learn one day to do better, we shall make ourselves judged by that hard word about the much speaking of the heathen—and this right in the midst of our churchly affairs. We are sufficiently familiar with the picture that presents itself at such occasions: Bible study with the coffee pot at hand, doughnuts, and the inevitable cigar. All this, presumably, because the Word of God has nothing to do with externals. Then, after a rich and bounteous supper, off to evening devotions, talking and discussing with each other about all sorts of things up to the very door of the chapel. If there is any place in Protestantism where the danger of magic threatens, then it is here where we expect spiritual experiences automatically to come about at such an *Unzeit*.

Wilhelm Stählin has recently put out a pertinent booklet in which he treats the "days set apart." He has worked out guidelines to be followed in free time and at conferences. They go from the minutest details of organization to fellowship with holy things— and all are informed of that which is timely and untimely. First of all it must be said that the man of our day cannot possibly turn from a lecture to a service of worship without an intervening period of quiet. In former times the Hours were observed and there was also a *statio* before all other meetings. This was observed by complete silence for about fifteen minutes before a service of worship or other proceedings. In fragments of the Rule of the Order of Knights this *statio* is expressly prescribed, for example, for all executive functions of the order. We, however, are still disposed to think that we can switch from discussion of duty to defend the country or from palaver about church taxes to things of worship and praise without a transitional exercise. This is obvious if one will observe the degree of attention that is given to such devotional periods. This has nothing to do with psychology or theology. It has everything to do with a palpable lack of love toward the human being of our day. In order to get out of this dilemma, we must produce an adequate evangelical breviary and this work has begun at varying theological fronts of our church.

It may be asked whether a leaf should not be taken from the

book of the Anglican Church so that instead of the routine morning and evening devotions there be a quiet time in which the individual is alone with his Bible. He may indeed spend this time of quiet in the company of others. The same holds for a time of silence after evening prayer. If after a day of exciting discussions one has experienced the boon of such silence in a disciplined way and without liturgical compulsion, he will never want to give it up. At this point we ought to question what seems to be held as the only proper way of conducting Bible studies. Every group of clergymen knows the feeling of distress when a certain participant asks for the floor, for they know a certain theological bent is sure to take the floor with him. It was once said, "When in our circuit brother X asks to speak I know exactly what he is going to say. But I do not have the faintest notion of how his wife fares or whether he has any trouble with his children." Such a sentence can rather easily be generalized.

In many instances something quite similar can be said of the sessions of our schools. It would seem that the method in which we have so largely done our Bible studies is pretty well passé. This does not say a thing against the Word of God. But it does say much against getting into ruts and against our predilection for outworn ways of doing things. The new consideration of the Word that was given us in the twenties must result in a rethinking of the character of the Word. And this revaluation will express itself at the place and at the time of the service of worship. The Preacher (Ecclesiastes) is right also when he says that there is a time and an *Unzeit* for everything.

The same laws hold for the time at which the liturgical service of worship is held. The fathers had different melodies for the parts of the liturgy when these were used at different times of the day. This was not by liturgical subtlety but by spiritual wisdom. *The Gloria Patri* has a different character in the morning service of prayer than it has when darkness comes with the night. In the morning the accent is on action and on readiness to achieve. This mood should move along with the morning prayer. At night, thoughts are different. Night is for rest, and its darkness is a harbinger of the shadows of death. However, these facts do not become evident if they are but rarely expressed at special meetings. If all services of worship are the same and if there is no hint of the rhythm of time in them, this similarity wearies the one who is intent upon observing morning, noon, and night as time of God in the rhythm of creation.

Similarly there is a difference between the liturgical parts of the Confession of Sins. Certainly, sin is always the same, having its roots in disobedience to God; but just as certainly, the temptations of the night are experienced on a different level than are those of the day. This realization is woven into the prayer for the night hour, not as some hybrid combination, but as an aid to one's soul.

The problem of right time and *Unzeit* can have significance for pastoral care. When this is seriously taken into account, the way is open to further the life of faith and to reach into questions on which decisions have to be made day by day. This is something more than a mere recognition of the problem in more or less correct liturgical procedure. Place and time are manipulated just as little as are other entities in creation. Whoever thinks that he may neglect them with impunity runs risks, as one does who tries to break through the God-willed rhythm in working. The neon light can make the night bright as day. And then we may surmise that we can work the night through as though it were day and suffer no impairment of health. But we have learned long ago that this is a conclusion by deception.

Only a few years ago we still thought that by means of chemicals we could effect untold yields from the soil. Today we wrestle with the problem of ever-increasing tissue diseases and wonder whether there may not be some connection between them and this chemical adulteration. It is only a matter of years since we hailed various antibiotics in pharmacology as wonder drugs. Now we face the ever-increasing problem with patients who have been treated with them from childhood and have developed such immunity to other medications that even overdoses of the wonder drugs are of no avail.

Now that we have rediscovered the Second Article which treats of redemption, we must pay equally discerning attention to creation treated of in the First Article. Does this not mean that, when we essay to render pastoral services to people, we must not deliberately go contrary to the creatural functions in the lives of people?

NOTES AND REFERENCES

Introduction

1. Consideration should be given to the critical remarks which Jaspers or Piccard have recently directed against the psychotherapeutic method. Compare my argument with Max Piccard on the psychotherapeutic method with children in *Quatember Heft Nr. 2/55*.

2. Compare Emil Brunner *Der Mensch im Widerspruch*, Chapter 16 *Seele und Leib*. Here it becomes clear that the relationship of the three concepts of soul, spirit, and body must not be given up. They designate the very nature of man. The passage cited from Luther's writings is in WA 7, 550.

3. In modern literature this concept was used for the first time as employed here in the *Festschrift* for Wilhelm Stählin, *Theologie und Kosmos*. From a survey of the several articles published there the term *Kosmische Theologie* has been chosen here. It can be misunderstood. *Kosmische Theologie*, of course, is Christocentric theology. At the same time it is theology which accords with the Trinity of God.

Part I—The Man to Whom We Proclaim

1. Compare here the foundation-laying works of Stern, *Psychologie der frühen Kindheit*, Pfahler, *Der Mensch und seine Vergangenheit*, and especially the works of Remplein, Bühler, and Hetzer. Anna Freud has also made significant contributions in her little book *Schwierige Kinder*.

2. For use of pastors and parents attention is called to a series of writings released by Verlag Ernst Klett, Stuttgart, *Bedrohte Jugend— Drohende Jugend*. About 40 issues are now available. They treat of educational problems in an easily understandable manner. These pamphlets

ought to be put into libraries of congregations. For specialized literature the works of Zulliger, Hanselmann, and Spieler are indicated. A book to be recommended as bridge between medicine and rearing at home is that of the Berlin pediatrician Anne Marie Dührsen, *Psychogene Erkrankungen bei Kindern und Jugendlichen (Verlag f. med. Psychologie, Göttingen).* The book by Otto Schlisske, *Evangelisches Elternbuch,* should be in the hands of all evangelical parents.

3. Besides, these titles are recommended: Kurt Seelmann, *Kind, Sexualität und Erziehung, Sexuelle Erziehung in Elternhaus und Schule,* reworked and published by Dr. Schimel and Karl Heinz Grothe. For young people the two little volumes by Dr. Bovet, Basel: *Von Mann zu Mann* and *Die werdende Frau* (both of Katzmann-Verlag, Tübingen), and the writings of Dr. Groeger under the title of *Mädchen, Liebe, Junge Männer,* Lätare-Verlag, Nürnberg. The pastor should not be without *Heft 10, Studienblätter für Evang. Jugendführung* which bears the title *Die Erziehung der Geschlechter.* Furthermore: Wilhelm Bitter's *Das Vaterproblem in Psychotherapie, Religion und Gesellschaft,* Hippokrates-Verlag, Stuttgart.

4. In 1926 Hildegard Hetzer put out an excellent study of the influence of the negative phase on the social attitude of girls in their puberty. It appeared in *Quellenstudien zur Jugendkunde,* Verlag Gustave Fischer, Jena, *Heft 4.*

5. Jörg Erb, *Die Wolke von Zeugen* and Walter Nigg, *Grosse Heilige* are suited to fill the gap in some measure.

6. It is over this question that controversy arises between psychology and pseudo-Christian ethics. In pastoral advice, judgments still are made which are medically false and tend to drive youth still more to masturbation. Compare Seelmann, *Kind, Sexualität und Erziehung,* pp. 127 ff. But especially the basic work of J. H. Schultz, *Organstörungen und Perversionen im Liebesleben.*

7. Compare Spieler, *Willensschwache werden willensstark,* Ernst Klett-Verlag, Stuttgart.

8. Here reference must be made to the early Christian mysticism of Dionysius the Areopagite, also to certain mystical strains that are discernible in early Orthodoxy and show up again in Berdyaev. What we have here are parallels in the history of religion which got into Christendom from the mystical religions. For particulars see *Augengott und heilige Hochzeit* by Margarete Riemschneider, Verlag Koehler-Amelang, Leipzig, particularly pp. 21 and 100 ff.

9. Matthew 22:30.

10. See in *Studienblätter für Evangelische Jugendführung,* Heft 11, *Jungen und Mädchen,* which is my treatment of the attracting and repulsing forces of the sexes from childhood to maturity.

11. With this compare Emil Brunner's book *Das Gebot und die Ordnungen,* Teil IV.

12. Karl Barth, *Dogmatik III,* 4 No. 54, pp. 127 f.

13. Bovet has said what needs to be said here in *Das Geheimnis ist gross,* Katzmann-Verlag, Tübingen.

Part II—Nature and Method of Our Proclamation

1. See *Über das Gespräch* by Albrecht Goes, Furche-Verlag, Hamburg, and *Heilung aus der Begegnung* by Hans Trüb, Ernst Klett-Verlag, Stuttgart.

2. Meanwhile the literature concerning confession has grown considerably, particularly in connection with the *Ev. Kirchentag,* 1955. Wilhelm Stählin's *Vom Sinne des Leibes,* 1929, has not been excelled to date; in it he demonstrated, probably for the first time, what possibilities there are in evangelical confession. Since then have come the treatments of the subject by Bernhard Ritter and, more recently, by Kurt Boehme. Also the works by Ruth Führer and Esther v. Kirchbach are still worth reading. In a summary way the whole development of the matter has been presented by Skydsgaard in the *Evangelisches Kirchenlexikon* under the title of *Beichte,* pp. 355 ff. Here there is also a bibliography. In it the book by Otto Händler, *Die Predigt,* merits special mention. Händler shows clearly the relationship between psychotherapy and private confession and assigns to each its particular function. The *Evang. Michaelis-Bruderschaft* has provided formulas for liturgical procedure for both private and congregational confession, available through the Johannes Stauda-Verlag, Kassel. The brotherhood has made practical use of them for 25 years.

3. Karl Bernhard Ritter, *Gebete für das Jahr der Kirche,* Joh. Stauda-Verlag, Kassel.

4. The mystery plays, which in Christendom are merely natural extensions of the Greek drama, are the last remnants of extra-cultic plays that have been preserved up to the end of the period of the Reformation. If we give a large place to proclamatory plays in the youth work of the church and marvel at the fact that the congregations are often moved more by the play than by the sermon, we begin to sense how great a role the mystery play had in the church's proclamation.

5. In his *Praktische Seelenkunde* (Ernst Reinhardt-Verlag, München), Richard Heyer seems to have come closest to wiping out the borderlines completely. This outstanding work by one of the fathers of psychotherapeutic practice in Germany could have devastating effects in the hands of theologians. In it practically every conflict in life is taken to be psychotherapeutically curable. In definite contrast to it the book that is to

be urgently recommended to pastors is one by the Berlin psychotherapist Dr. Hans March, *Lebensschicksale in psychiatrischen Gutachten,* Ferdinand Enke-Verlag, Stuttgart, 1954. In both instances the authors are eminent authorities in their subject. March sees a borderline of psychotherapy; Heyer has the eros of healing go across the borderline; in fact, he does not allow a borderline at all. We do not state this as an appraisal but simply as a disclosure of the tension that prevails within psychotherapy. Compare especially: Martin Buber's *Schuld und Schuldgefühle* in *Merkur,* August 1957.

6. Taken from R. Brun's *Neurosenlehre.*

7. By phobia is meant a condition of fear for which there is no evident background. Freud contrasts it with real fear or fear of living. Fear of a snake is real fear, because the snake represents a threat to my existence. Fear of mice is a phobia, because there is no reasonable ground for fearing a mouse that does not threaten one's life. Phobias in every case have in their background either the individual's psychical experiences or are parts of the individual's fear of our human existence in general.

8. The further development of this takes place preeminently in the school of the neo-analysts (Schultz-Henke). Fränkel of Vienna and particularly Künkel bring in a degree of limitation. Among the modern critics of a radical sort Jaspers and Max Piccard can be mentioned.

9. R. S. Lee, *Freud and Christianity.* James Clark & Co., Ltd., and *Psychology and Worship.*

10. Even a theologian like Walter Uhsadel succumbs to this temptation when he attempts to give a pastoral exposition of the Parable of the Lost Son on basis of Jungian ideas in his little book *Der Mensch und die Mächte des Unbewussten,* Joh. Stauda-Verlag, 1952.

11. Here we should make mention of C. G. Jung's archetypes. These are notions that control the essence of man. They are revealed in tales, dreams, and religious symbolism. They are really the basis for the understanding of Jung's psychology. Otto Haendler has worked with keen insight on their relationship to each other in his book *Die Predigt* (Verlag Töpelmann, Berlin) and *Angst und Glaube* (Evang. Verlagsanstalt, Berlin).

12. Compare the controversy between Schätzing, Berlin, and Bovet, Basel, in *Wege zum Menschen,* 7. Jahrgang, 1955, Heft Nr. 4 & 9.

13. See *Agape* in *Theologisches Wörterbuch zum Neuen Testament.*

14. Werner Elert has proved the correctness of this ancient saying *lex orandi-lex credendi* in his *Abendmahl und Gemeinschaft der alten Kirche, hauptsächlich des Ostens.* On page 91 he writes, "In the ancient church there is no dogma that does not have liturgical quality." Again, on page 93, "In the ancient church dogma is intended to be confession;

in its substance it carries the creed of the primitive church, and creed stands for congregation." Similar views are expressed by Cullmann and Peter Brunner. Compare also *Credo Ecclesiam*, John Stauda-Verlag 1955.

15. The significance of the picture is demonstrated especially in the life of an artist. For he is predominantly a *visile*, and in his creative efforts he draws chiefly on the imaginal layer of his mind. The question may be asked whether such a one can feel at home in Protestantism with its cultural shape. This is not asked in view of the ranking writers and poets who have become converts in our day. Since the time of the Reformation proper there has hardly been any genuinely Protestant art that is worth mentioning. (Rembrandt is no proof to the contrary!) When Erhardt Kästner, who for many years was private secretary to Gerhart Hauptmann, writes in his *Zeltbuch von Tumilad*, he speaks for many. "Pictures! pictures! Of what use are thoughts? art? knowledge? doctrines and great systems? It is by pictures that the soul renews itself. So it has been since primitive time. What grows out of insight, experience, presentiment, and knowledge must become a picture, or it is dead. One has total possession of the truth only when he has it in a picture. Only he who holds things in a picture owns them" (pages 68-69).

16. Lamentations 3:41; Psalm 141:2; Isaiah 1:15; 1 Timothy 2:8.

17. Compare Karl Ferdinand Müller *Die Neuordnung des Gottesdienstes in Theologie und Kirche*, Joh. Stauda, Kassel.

18. Extensive works on the nature of Christian meditation are not extant. We know that Luther used such books of meditation as were available to him. One dissertation on the subject that appeared shortly before the war was destroyed in the war. The author, Erich Sander, Ph.D., of Essen did not return from the war. Thus there are two booklets on the subject that continue to be the most basic. One is *Über die Meditation als Mittel der Menschbildung* by the theologian K. B. Ritter and *Anleitung zur Meditation* by the lamented physician Dr. Carl Happich. Other works, like those of Friso Melzer, Kurt Irmler, and others come dangerously near to being speculative considerations, or they approach views that are influenced by the thought of Rudolf Stainer. A modern and truly comprehensive work on Christian meditation as spiritual exercise is still lacking. A generally understandable introduction to Xen- (or Zen-) Buddhism is Alan W. Watts's *Vom Geist der Zen*, Benno Schwabe Verlag, Basel. Compare also *Grundriss der praktischen Theologie* by Haendler, pp. 119-129.

19. At the International World Congress on *Liturgie und Pastoral*, 1956 in Assisi, the Augustinian Father Agostino Bea gave a report on *Die seelsorgerliche Bedeutung des Wortes Gottes in der Liturgie*, which has attracted much attention. In it statements are made that are quite in

line with Protestant theological teaching on the nature of the Word of God. Of the biblical books it is said, "I do intentionally say that they are God's Word; they do not merely contain God's Word as does the Catechism or an instruction book on religion. They are God's Word through the particular *charisma* of inspiration, by which God has eternal truth employ the services of a human writer with all his capacities in a veritable one-time manner." Truly exciting is what is said in Section 3 under the caption *Das Wort Gottes in Verbindung mit dem eucharistischen Opfer*. This article is proof that earnest, influencial groups in the Roman Church are at work to discover relationship to the Word. Particulars are in *Herder-Korrespondenz*, Jahrgang 11, Heft 3, Dec. 1956, pp. 137-139.

20. Compare *Quatember*, Jahrgang 56/57, Heft 1: Friedemann Gottschick, *Neue Wege in der Psalmodie*. Furthermore, compare the phonograph records of worship services at Taizé-Les-Cluny of the Parisian Firma Studio SM. The so-called Gelineau-Psalms have been developed further by Gerhard Schwarz in the *Untermühle* by Imshausen. This is chiefly a home for children. The Psalm compositions by Schwarz are regularly used there in midday prayer.

21. In psychological testing this fact is used in the tree test. In the way and manner in which a person draws a tree it can be determined what kind of capabilities he may have, but also what difficulties and inclinations he may have. In our connection it is of interest to note that this is not possible with just any object, but that this comes about precisely in the sketching of a tree. Particulars are given by Karl Koch in *Der Baumtest*, Verlag Hans Huber, Bern and Stuttgart, specifically on pages 24-32.

Part III—The Place Where We Proclaim

1. Langmaack, *Leiturgia I*, pp. 380 ff.

2. Hans Sedlmayr, *Verlust der Mitte*, particularly Chapters 3, 4 and 13.

3. More on this in my article *Die seelsorgerliche Atmosphäre* in *Wege zum Menschen*, Jahrg. 6, Heft 2.

Part IV—The Time When We Proclaim

1. Here compare especially Hans Blüher, *Die Achse der Natur*, Chapters 2 and 10. The lie is here given to the myth that there are no presuppositions in mathematics. Proof is given that the conformity to law that prevails in the cosmos is the a priori of time and number. Plumbed to its depth this conformity to law is of the Trinity of God. Blüher also shows that the concept of mathematics varies as it is thought through by

the Egyptians on the one hand and by the Greeks on the other hand. By this concept of the axis of nature *(Naturachse)* Blüher accords a place to number in natural cosmical event.

2. This mathematical dialectic on the bounds of the infinite emerges as clearly from the possibility of the nth power ($a^n=0$) as from the fact that the fourth dimension is a quantity that can be calculated but is not conceivable as an entity.

3. Such thoughts raise the question as to the degree of attention biblical theology should pay to anthroposophic lines of thinking. What separates us from the assertion by Rudolf Steiner is the simple fact that our interest is always in the Christ of Golgotha and Easter, that is, in the *Christus Incarnatus,* in *Christus natus ex Maria virgine.* So long as anthroposophy dissolves the historic Christ and degrades him to a docetic bearer of a semblance of a body there is no bridge for us to it. In the last analysis anthroposophy is just another of the many deviations that arose because of a vacuum when the church could no longer bear witness to the *Christus Incarnatus* in the cosmos. We mean, therefore, to be rendering the church a service when we draw the lines of the incarnation into the concepts of space, number, and time.

4. Gregory Dix, *The Shape of the Liturgy,* Chapter XI, *The Sanctification of Time.*

5. The available material that is historical in character and is related to the history of dogma on the fixing of the time for worship has been gathered by Dr. G. Kunze in *Leiturgia II,* in *Die gottesdienstliche Zeit.* The passages cited here are from this essay.

6. Compare again *Leiturgia II,* pp. 460 ff.

7. *Die Klosterregel des Heiligen Benedikt,* Beuroner Kunstverlag 1952.

8. Indeed, he did compose noonday prayers, and he also collected a selection of definite prayers and Psalms for that hour. When it comes to Luther's position on the Hours it must not be forgotten that abuse beclouded use for him in his day. As far as we know, Luther himself did observe the Hours. But in the situation of his day he could not recommend the practice to his congregation because Roman tradition of the time had made for the emptying of personal prayer. A more extensive treatment of Luther's attitude toward the Hours is in the essay by Herbert Goltzen, *Der tägliche Gottesdienst, Leiturgia III,* pp. 187 ff. In any case, the Hours are the property also of Reformed Christians. Schmidt-Klausing has shown to what degree regulated prayer originally belonged to the Reformed tradition—this in his book *Zwingli als Liturgiker.*

9. The real beginning of the new order of things was made in the twenties of our century with the *Gebet der Tageszeiten* of the *Evangelische Michaelis-Bruderschaft.* After this came *Das Stundengebet,*

and for the service at the altar the agenda of K. B. Ritter, *Gebete der Kirche*. The *Pfarrgebete* may also be mentioned. Besides these there are a number of useful prayer booklets in modern literature, particularly the *Evangelische Gebetbuch* for student congregations. The fact must not be overlooked that additional prayers in the *EKG* (hymnbook) represent a good impetus to the recovery of aids for congregations in the use of formulated prayers.

10. Emil Brunner, *Das Gebot und die Ordnungen*, pp. 47 ff. and 481 ff.

11. Augsburg Confession, Articles 7 & 8 *De Ecclesia*. Large Catechism, *De sacramento altaris*, "Even though a knave take or distribute the sacrament, he receives the true sacrament, that is, the true body and blood of Christ, just as truly as he who receives or administers it in the most worthy manner. . . . This is as much as to say, No matter whether you be worthy or unworthy, you have here his body and blood by virtue of these words which are added to the bread and wine" (Translation by H. E. Jacobs).